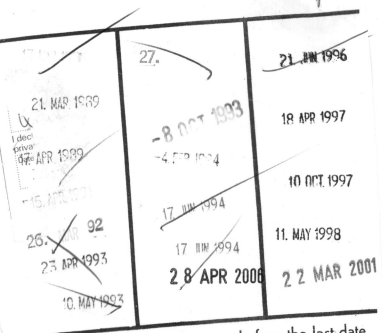

PER ANGER

With Raoul Wallenberg in Budapest

Memories of the War Years in Hungary

PREFACE BY ELIE WIESEL

*Translated from the Swedish
by David Mel Paul and Margareta Paul*

HOLOCAUST LIBRARY
NEW YORK

Cover design by Michael Meyerowitz
Printed in the United States of America
by Waldon Press Inc., New York

To Raoul

"An eternal glory surrounds his name and his memory. The refugee organization of the United States has also expressed its admiration for his achievement, which is called one of this war's greatest individual performances."

(From an editorial in Svenska Dagbladet, April 22, 1945)

Contents

A Few Words About
Raoul Wallenberg

By ELIE WIESEL

Raoul Wallenberg remains a living legend for the Jews of Budapest. Few have done what he did to save them. No one could claim more daring adventures and greater success. He set an example that only few have followed.

Read this book and you will see that although pursued and hunted, many victims could have escaped the killers. Many could have been saved. Death trains *were* turned back. Prisoners *were* freed. In some cases, Eichmann and his aides were forced to yield, and did release their prey. What was needed then was only some measure of good will, decency and courage, skills and means, and a bit of imagination — what was needed was the desire to get involved on the side of suffering humanity, on the side of the Jews.

Read this book and you will reach the shocking and painful conclusion that victory over the killers was possible. This was true of both private citizens and officials, of individuals and governments alike: throughout the kingdom of night, wherever a person or a family chose to oppose the executioner and hide his victims, death was defeated.

Sadly, tragically, Raoul Wallenberg belonged to a minority, a small minority. And his mission started late, much too late, at a time when, except for those in the Hungarian capital, there were no more Jews left to be saved.

Why had he not been sent earlier? Why had other diplomats not been dispatched to other cities, on similar rescue operations? What would have happened if, in 1943, neutral nations had offered protection to the Jews of Warsaw, if great powers had offered citizenship to the Jews of Paris and Amsterdam?

You read the story of Raoul Wallenberg and you are overcome by feelings of both gratitude and sadness: gratitude to the young Swedish diplomat and his friends, and sadness towards all the others, on account of the others.

You read what was accomplished by a handful of men and women, and you try to imagine what could have been accomplished if more people had shown that they cared! You think of missed opportunities and lost chances; you think of the prolonged silence of the Allied leaders, and your melancholy approaches despair.

For this cruelest of catastrophes could have been averted, or at least diminished. We know it now; we should have guessed it then. If only certain gates had been open to Jewish refugees; if only certain governments had been willing to save Jewish children; if only certain leaders had protested against the massacres when they first occurred; if only proper warnings had been issued to the German people about post-war retribution for Auschwitz and Treblinka — if only . . . No wonder that Hitler and Himmler, Heydrich and Eichmann interpreted the attitude of the western powers as tacit consent if not outright encouragement! The Nazi leaders were convinced that, in getting rid of Europe's undesirable Jews, they were rendering a true service to humanity.

When, after the torment, leaders of the free world said "We did not know," they were not telling the truth. They knew. Others stated that they knew but were powerless to do anything; they were not telling the truth either. They were not powerless. The best proof: Raoul Wallenberg.

Read this book about him — and other books as well: Jacques Derogy's "Le Cas Wallenberg," Eleanore Lester's essay on him in *The New York Times Magazine* — and you will see what one man could do: he could provide inspiration and hope to an entire community.

Granted, his successes should not be exaggerated; he did not fight alone. He had allies, colleagues, friends; he had the support of influential people in Stockholm and Washington. With equal heroism and devotion the Swiss consul — Charles Lutz, a legendary figure in his own right — took part in the same struggle, as did the Apostolic Nuncio Angelo Rotta and other diplomats from neutral countries. And, above all, we must not forget the young Zionists. They fought the enemy day and night, with rare if not unique bravery and ingenuity, outwitting him again and again, using ruse as much as weaponry to snatch from him a man here, a family there . . . These young lions, often disguised as members of the Fascist movement, managed to save many lives.

But the great hero was Raoul Wallenberg; he was the symbol, the flame. Is that the reason why the Russians arrested him? Is that why they have kept him in prison and still refuse to release him? So long as a

Raoul Wallenberg exists, oppressive systems will be exposed and condemned. Wallenberg will forever testify for man's need to remain human and his ability to succeed. That is why we wish to see him free — so as to thank him — thank him for enabling us, through his work and sacrifice, to proclaim our faith in human solidarity, even when the surrounding world trembled in fear and celebrated hate and death.

I do not know what place Raoul Wallenberg occupies in the history of his people; but I do know the place he occupies in ours: it is a place reserved for a man embodying our thirst for justice and dignity, and above all our quest for humanity.

Apologue de RW

Foreword

Some years after the end of the war, Gunnar Hägglöf, then the Swedish ambassador in London, said to me: "Why don't we, who were there, write a book together about the foreign service officer's experiences in the Second World War?"

Sven Grafström, Kurt Allan Belfrage, Carl Douglas and Hugo Ärnfast were also to take part, writing about events as they experienced them in Poland, Rumania, Norway and Berlin, respectively.

For various reasons, the book never came about. During the years that followed, three of its intended authors died — Grafström, Douglas and Ärnfast. They had made it through the bombs and grenades of war but lost their lives in accidents in other parts of the world.

As for me, I have hesitated to publish my experiences of the war in Hungary. Originally, they were conceived as part of a larger story, in which my deceased comrades, too, would have wielded the pen.

My collaboration with Raoul Wallenberg in the rescue operation of the Hungarian Jews during the war drew us together. His fate has come more and more to occupy my thoughts. For this reason, I have expanded my original chapter in an attempt to describe what happened and what should have been done from the Swedish side — especially at an early stage — to rescue Raoul.

Per Anger
Stockholm, August 1979

The German Occupation

It was Sunday morning, the 19th of March, 1944, in Budapest. At six in the morning I was wakened by a telephone call from my chief, Minister Ivan Danielsson.

"The Germans are taking over the city. Come to the legation at once!"

What we had long expected now took place with lightning speed.

It was widely known that the Germans did not trust Hungary as an ally but feared that one sunny day the country would go looking for a way to "jump ship." The worse it went for Germany on the eastern front, the more the Hungarians wavered. The Germans had long mistrusted the Hungarian prime minister, Miklós Kállay. This was because he had declared publicly on several occasions that Hungary had been forced into the war against her will — needless to say, by the Germans.

Through his tightrope-walking policy, Kállay attempted, at one and the same time, to maintain correct relations with Germany, barring the way to further German demands and, behind the Germans' backs, to keep the door open for negotiations with the Allies, primarily the Americans and English.

The Hungarians anticipated the approach of Russian occupation with great anxiety and hoped to the very end that American and British troops would get there first. They even dreamed of being able to throw out the Germans, declare Hungary neutral, and thereby avoid occupation.

As a Hungarian patriot, Kállay had but one goal in mind: to keep the country intact as long as possible and to be able, at the inevitable showdown that was approaching, to hold on to as much as possible of Hungary's resources, territorial gains and social and political system.

The contacts with the Allies were made chiefly in Istanbul and Stockholm by special emissaries. In Istanbul the intermediary was, among others, Nobel prizewinner Albert Szent-Györgi, as will be described later. In Stockholm, at first, a Hungarian journalist, Andor Gellért, carried out Kállay's instructions. There he had contact mostly with the American legation.

I came to know Gellért during a visit to Stockholm. He related to me that he had been sent to Berlin in 1938 as contact man for the then prime minister, Paul Teleki. There he became good friends with several of the American embassy staff. When the United States entered the war, these American diplomats were moved to Stockholm and Gellért followed, to keep in touch with them. He had also been asked by the Hungarian Social Democratic Party to keep in touch with the Swedish Social Democrats and with the British Labor Party. Thereby, he came in contact with Vilmos Böhm, a Hungarian radical leftist who had earlier been a member of Béla Kun's Communist government. Böhm lived as a refugee in Stockholm, where he worked as a translator for a British news agency. After the war, Böhm was appointed the Hungarian minister in Stockholm.

In the autumn of 1943, Gellért received instructions to pass on the following to the Americans:

1. Hungary did not intend to make any resistance whatsoever, should British or American forces invade the country.

2. Hungary was, in principle, prepared to end up on the Allied side against the Germans if a plan could be worked out for joint action.

3. The object of such a plan would not be to save the Hungarian government but only to try to assure the future of the Hungarian people.

It later became evident that the Germans, through their spies, had been able to follow these moves of the Hungarian government.

Thus it was not surprising that the Germans now struck. One may well wonder why they had not done so long before.

Meanwhile, the people of Budapest lived on, without the least notion of what was coming. Most of them rejoiced at the Allied victories and at the speed with which the war seemed to be ending. March was the month of festivals, and parties blossomed as never before. In Budapest's restaurants nothing was lacking, and in the evenings one strolled along the Korzo by the Danube while the gypsy orchestras played their caressing, traditional melodies. It was as if there had never been any war.

The celebration of the national holiday on the 15th of March, 1944, was prepared for as usual. On the 20th, there would be an even greater festivity because of the 50th anniversary of the death of Hungary's national hero, Lajos Kossuth. Parliament would meet on that day, and Kállay would make an important speech. The rumor was spread that he would then announce Hungary's surrender and the arrival of airborne British and American troops.

But fate ruled otherwise. Kállay would never again make a speech to the Hungarian nation.

The national holiday arrived, and the grand climax of the celebration was to be the premiere of a new patriotic opera, "Petöfi."

Regent and "Administrator of the Realm" Nicholas Horthy and his wife attended the event, along with a large flock of Hungarian celebrities. It was Mme. Horthy's first public appearance since the tragic death of their eldest son Istvan, a fighter pilot on the eastern front whose plane crashed. I went with Danielsson to the opera. Between the acts, one of the attachés at the German embassy confided to me that his chief, Minister von Jagow, had just given Horthy an important message from Hitler. Later we learned that the message was a summons to Hitler's headquarters, a prelude to the occupation.

Making my way to the legation early on Sunday morning the 19th of March, I saw the first German soldiers on Budapest's streets. Some hours later, from Gellért Hill where the legation was located, we could watch the German armored columns rolling into the city. Silent and grave, the inhabitants of Budapest watched the course of events.

It now became public that Regent Horthy had been "invited" the day before to Hitler's headquarters in Klessheim castle outside Salzburg for "discussions." This was a pattern Hitler had successfully followed earlier, when he summoned Austria's Schuschnigg and Czechoslovakia's Hácha to see him in 1938 and 1939, respectively.

This was Horthy's second visit to Hitler in a year. At the previous meeting, in April 1943, he had received a list of Hitler's demands and complaints against Hungary, as follows:

1. The Hungarians had fought badly on the eastern front and had sabotaged the joint war efforts. Still more Hungarian troops must now be put at Germany's disposal.

2. The Hungarian standard of living was too high. The economy was to be organized for total war and production directed toward providing for Germany's needs.

3. The Hungarian Jews still had far too much freedom. Actions must be taken to solve the Jewish problem once and for all.

4. Leftist groups in Hungary had been treated too mildly. It was especially important that the Social Democratic Party be dissolved.

5. Germany had indisputable evidence that someone on the Hungarian side had been in touch with the British and American governments. Such contacts would have to cease, and the press chief of the Hungarian foreign ministry, Antal Ullein-Reviczky, who had played one of the leading roles in these approaches to the Allies, should be dismissed.* Prime Minister Kállay should be replaced by someone who

* It can now be told that the mission, specifically Danielsson and, in his absence, I, maintained especially close contact with Ullein-Reviczky. He belonged to the pro-Allied group in the foreign ministry. The Germans were right in their judgment of him.

was prepared to put all the Hungarian forces into the war on the eastern front.

The old Regent became mightily incensed at these complaints. He found it especially hard to swallow Hitler's disparaging remarks about the Hungarian troops. The view generally held in Hungary was that, in the fighting on the eastern front, the Germans had left the Hungarians in the lurch, and that, with insufficient equipment, they were forced to form a rear guard to cover the German retreat.

Consequently, Horthy refused to accede to the five German demands and returned in a fury from the first meeting. However, after the second meeting on March 19, 1944, Hitler — having repeated his demands — took the matter into his own hands. Horthy was detained against his will while "Operation Margarethe" — prepared long before — was set in motion.

Hungary was occupied, following the well-tested recipe, in a single morning. The border was overrun with swift motorized units, while parachute troops secured airports and other strategic points in the country.

In Budapest, all official buildings, radio and telegraph stations were quickly invested by German forces. Kállay's regime was deposed and replaced by a government friendly to the Germans, with the Hungarian ambassador to Berlin, General Sztójay, as prime minister. His first act was to make sure that the Hungarian army, most of which happened to be at the Rumanian border, offered no resistance. Named to head the most important ministry, that of the Interior, were the former major of police Baky and the governor of Pest, Endre. Both were known for their fanatical anti-Semitism, and both belonged to the Hungarian Nazi party, the so-called Arrow Cross party.

Mass arrests of suspected persons were undertaken with the help of Germans who, in various guises, had resided in Budapest before the occupation, in collusion with the Arrow Cross.

The surprise was total, and Hungary capitulated without a struggle that Sunday. Everywhere there were traitors. Perhaps the most typical example was Horthy's own private detective, Peter Hain, who now revealed himself as the Germans' man and after a time was appointed head of the secret police. Through Hain, who had had Horthy's complete confidence, it had been possible for the Germans to follow the Hungarian leadership's moves day by day and thereby to decide the most auspicious day for their own occupation.

The Germans did their work according to a carefully prepared plan. Their first act was to seize persons known as anti-Nazis: leading politicians, officials and scientists, industrialists and businessmen. The minister of the Interior, Keresztes-Fischer, was arrested. Kállay escaped arrest by the skin of his teeth and succeeded in making his way to the Turkish legation. The Germans went from house to house, taking hostages, checking off a list. But this list was quite out of date. That is, it included the names of some persons who had already been dead several years, something that shows that the German "master race" had already long before thought about taking over Hungary!

Ullein-Reviczky, the chief of press relations in the foreign ministry whose dismissal Hitler had demanded, was no longer in Hungary. By the fall of 1943 he had been appointed minister to Sweden and was in Stockholm. There, at Kállay's bidding, he had followed up on the contacts initiated by Gellért and negotiated with the Allied missions on a separate peace for Hungary. However, these negotiations had not led anywhere, since those on the Allied side demanded unconditional surrender to all three allies. The Hungarians might consider capitulating to the British and American forces, but not to the Russian. Actually, all the Hungarian attempts to surrender unilaterally to the western Allies were doomed to fail from the start. It was not the Hungarians who got to choose their conquerors. What Kállay did not know, when he based his policy on Englishmen and Americans freeing his country, was that the three allies had decided in Teheran in November 1943 that eastern Europe would be the Red Army's territory of operations.

After the German occupation, Ullein-Reviczky resigned as official Hungarian representative in Sweden, but was given the Swedish government's permission to remain as a private person with unimpaired diplomatic privileges. During the last years of the war, he worked vigorously for the creation of "Free Hungary" in other countries.

Hitler's hand-picked "Plenipotentiary of the Greater German Reich in Hungary," Dr. Veesenmayer, now moved into the German legation in Budapest. During some months disastrous for Hungary, he would be the most powerful man in the country. The rumor of his cruel ravages in Yugoslavia, where he had earlier worked as Hitler's special emissary, had preceded his arrival.

A special unit headed by Adolf Eichmann was set up, its assignment the final solution of the Jewish problem in Hungary. Eichmann brought with him few but ruthless henchmen: Krumey, Hunsche, Dannecker and Wisliceny. As additional help, Eichmann had Otto Klages from the SS security service, who had the assignment of concealing the operation against the Jews and the goal of the deportations. The SS security service had long been in sharp opposition to the German armed forces' security organization under Admiral Canaris.

Thus the Hungarians, and especially Hungary's Jews, entertained no illusions about what was at hand.

Authentic descriptions of liquidations of Jews in Poland's gas chambers or in other ways had already reached Budapest. I myself heard the following from a Hungarian journalist, Kálmán Konkoly, who returned at the end of 1942 from the war in Russia. On one occasion, he had been witness to how five thousand Jews, after being forced to dig their own graves, were mowed down with machine guns by two German soldiers. Afterward, he had encountered the soldiers at the inn, in the Russian village where they had been stationed. One of them, apparently very musical, sat playing Beethoven on the house piano. They related that they were teachers in civilian life and that they were proud of having done a deed that day that served humanity by contributing to exterminating the Jews!

Now we tensely awaited Horthy's next move when

he returned from Klessheim. It was already too late to order the Hungarian Army to resist. All that came of his threat of resignation was that Veesenmayer came to the Castle and laid his cards on the table. Veesenmayer had been dubbed "Reichsverveesenmayer" in Hungarian anti-Nazi circles — a pun upon the fact that it was he who held the real power in Hungary, and not *Reichsverweser* (Administrator of the Realm) Horthy. He now stated that, should Horthy resign, Hungary would be incorporated into Germany as a protectorate, as had already happened to Czechoslovakia and Poland.

Horthy faced a difficult choice. Of course he could have committed suicide like the Hungarian prime minister, Paul Teleki. In the spring of 1941, Teleki took his own life because of the betrayal of Yugoslavia when the Germans were granted free passage through Hungary to attack that country. However, Horthy's death would not improve the situation but instead further strengthen the Germans' position. It has been said that it was the Danish king's conduct on the 9th of April, 1940, that Horthy took as his model when he decided to stay at his post and accept Sztójay's government. It is also probable that Horthy regarded that government as the lesser evil and that, rather than resign, he would remain to hinder the takeover of power by the Arrow Cross. He made no secret of regarding the Arrow Cross leader, Ferenc Szálasi, as a great scoundrel and traitor.

In April, some weeks after the German occupation, our daughter was born. I had just driven my wife Elena to the hospital and returned to the legation when the air raid alarm went off. We all knew what that meant: the Allies' answer to the German occupation of Budapest. I defied the ban on going outdoors and drove back to the hospital. Our daughter was born before the attack actually came. Only minutes before the bombs fell, the new-born babies and their parents were brought in safety to the shelter. Between the bombings we succeeded in making arrangements for a subsequent christening at the legation. The officiant at the christening was the Lutheran minister, Wolf Ordas, who earlier had studied under the renowned Swedish theologian, Nathan Söderblom. He became one of the most important bulwarks in the Hungarian resistance to Nazism and after the war was made bishop of Budapest.

The first American bombing attacks were directed only at military targets and war industries. In full daylight, the American planes flew over the city in waves, releasing their bombs with unfailing precision upon the railyards, the Manfred-Weiss works and the oil refineries on Csepel Island in the Danube. From the roof of the bunker in the legation garden, we could follow the drama, a hint of what was to come. One day, apparently by mistake, one bomb fell on the Gellért Hotel that lay just below us and smashed in all the windows of our legation building. After that, we no longer stood outside watching, unnecessarily, once the air raid signal went off. The air attacks increased in severity every day and now not only military targets were being attacked. One day a "carpet" of bombs was laid along the great Andrássy Boulevard, which ran east and west through the Pest section of the city, leveling some of the city's most elegant residential quarters. After that, the legation seriously urged all Swedes who were not absolutely constrained to remain, to leave the country.

Hungarian Moods

In Budapest, people had not yet been deeply affected by the war. True, the collapse on the Don front at Voronezh, in January 1943, when the Hungarians lost almost five divisions in dead and wounded, had left deep scars. But, in general, life in the capital went on as before. Actions such as rationing and blackouts, which reminded people that Hungary was, in spite of everything, at war, had been taken — but mostly for form's sake. Hungary was a fertile agricultural country that did not suffer any lack of food and one that had been almost completely spared any enemy air attack.

In our spare time, we sometimes took part in hunting trips that our Hungarian friends arranged. The country was rich in wild game and, even if I was not among the most enthusiastic of hunters, it proved a welcome supplement when I could bring home a rabbit or two to extend our rationed diet.

One day, my wife and I were invited by the lawyer, Miklós von Kállay, a distant relative of the then prime minister, to Transylvania on the Rumanian border for a bear hunt. I accepted with hesitation, since I had no experience in hunting big game. Early on the morning of the hunt, we were fortified with a typical Transylvanian breakfast consisting of home-baked coarse bread, bacon with paprika, hot milk and "barack," the Hungarian apricot brandy. Then I was put on watch in a grove of trees. My host pointed out the direction from which the bear might be expected to come. I stood there on shaky legs, praying that no bear would come my way, and luckily my wish was granted.

Twenty years later, I met von Kállay in Los Angeles, where he had come as a refugee after the war. While he sat and chatted about old times, the bear hunt came up. I asked him, half joking, how he could have risked my life by leaving me alone on watch for a Transylvanian bear, which isn't one of the smaller ones! If a bear had appeared, wouldn't I have come out second best? He laughed and replied: "There was no danger. You didn't know it, but I had placed my best shots in the trees all around you!"

In the legation, the daily work went on as usual. Our cultural exchange with Hungary flourished at that time. Swedish opera singers visited Budapest. Jussi Björling, Joel Berglund, Einar Beyron and Brita Herzberg were celebrated guest artists at the Budapest Opera and no one was more popular than Set Svanholm, with his Wagner performances.

The soccer tournament in the summer of 1943 was a disappointment for the Hungarians, since the Swedes won. My wife and I attended the game with Danielsson. Horthy sat in front of us in the official box. In the beginning, he was sunny as could be, while luck was with the Hungarians. But when, in the second half, the Swedes took the lead, the old admiral clouded over and departed without a word.

Most of the daily work at the legation had to do with trade and included making sure that the Hungarians fulfilled their commitments to Sweden, delivering the desired commodities on time. Several industrial and food products important to the support of our country in wartime were involved. The interest our Swedish supply commissions expressed in Hungary, at this season, mostly concerned the question of whether turkeys and apples would get to us by Christmas, and eggs by Easter.

There were bilateral negotiations under idyllic conditions in that last stage before the collapse. We became good friends with our Hungarian negotiating partners. When we asked them about the future, they would only reply: "Look at our history! We have made it through the ravages of the Huns, 150 years of Turkish subjugation, domination by Austria, and now the Germans, tomorrow the Russians! *Nem, nem soha* (No, no, never) is the slogan you encounter everywhere you go in Hungary, a slogan coined after the First World War's unjust Trianon Peace. Hungary was maimed, and we had to give up 70 per cent of our land area to our greedy neighbors. We have a hopeless strategic geography, being on a plain at the boundary between east and west, open to attack from all sides. But we're going to survive!"

Their relations with neighboring countries were still marked with great mistrust, and they allowed themselves no illusions about getting to keep, in the long run, those areas they had regained with the help of the Germans. An aversion to Rumania in particular was evident among Hungarians in general. I felt this strongly while conversing with people during a trip into eastern Hungary with a group of Swedish journalists. An answer that a farmer gave one of these journalists, Erik Wästberg, editor in chief of the *Nya*

Dagligt Allehanda, was illuminating. He asked the farmer what he thought of Sweden. "It's a wonderful country," the farmer said. "Why do you think so?" asked Wästberg. "Because it's so far away!" was the answer.

The Swedish Mission's
First Rescue Operations

The German takeover meant that the Swedish legation was faced with new, difficult problems. During his conversation with Horthy on the day before the occupation, Hitler had once again demanded vigorous efforts against the Hungarian Jews. True, the Hungarians had already introduced their Jewish ordinances, under the influence of both the Germans and strong anti-Semitic forces in the country. These were primarily intended to reduce the number of Jews in public service and in the independent professions, and to limit their activity in commercial, industrial and banking enterprises. But according to the Germans these regulations were not enough. Their view was that Hungary had shown its inability to come to grips with the problem and that 800,000 Jews in the country, of whom 200,000 resided in Budapest, could become a dangerous fifth column in the rear of the German army.

Within a few days of the occupation, they began arresting Jews in prominent positions. At the legation, we were all indirectly affected, for many of our Jewish friends were involved. Most often, we knew only that they had disappeared.

When we first came to Budapest, my wife and I had rented a place in a house on Gellért Hill that belonged to Baron Alfonse Weiss. He and his family owned the well-known Manfred-Weiss factories on Csepel Island between Buda and Pest. Weiss also had extensive property in the Hungarian countryside and was regarded as one of Hungary's wealthiest and most influential Jewish men, belonging to a family who had played an important role in the country's economic and cultural life. In the same house, an older Jewish couple also lived.

A few days after the Germans' entry into Budapest, this couple disappeared without a trace. Rumor had it that they were victims of the first German wave of arrests. Rumor was right. When I learned, after an intensive search, that they had been taken to a camp on the outskirts of Budapest, I went there. I was able to establish that they, along with about a hundred other unfortunates, found themselves behind barbed wire, awaiting transport to Poland's gas chambers.

Their resignation before this fate was evident. This was my first confrontation with the Nazi executioner state.

Many harrowing experiences would follow.

We became witnesses to something we had not thought possible in modern times: the beginning of a systematic extermination of a whole race. In various cases, desperate measures were taken to save Jews in our circle of acquaintances. A Swedish businessman declared himself ready to marry a Jewish woman who had been arrested. Someone tried to hide Jewish friends in his house or hire them pro forma as servants. But nothing helped. Those who were on the SS list when the Germans entered the city were hunted down and taken away, almost without exception.

The legation's channel for action was through the

Hungarian Foreign Ministry which was, however, powerless in the prevailing situation. One family succeeded in saving itself, that is, the aforementioned Alfonse Weiss and his relatives. A member of the family, Ferenc Chorin, who was said to be the "brains" of the Manfred-Weiss firm, had been arrested when the Germans came in. He was taken to Vienna but negotiated his way to freedom for himself and his family. Cleverly, he played upon the rivalry between Goering and Himmler's SS. He offered to sell the Manfred-Weiss factories to Himmler in return for a safe-conduct for 48 members of the Weiss family. The SS supplied them with appropriate travel documents, including false Portuguese visas, and a cash sum of $600,000 dollars, and flew them to Portugal, where they found sanctuary. However, three of the family members were kept in Vienna as hostages to guarantee that those freed did not "take part in any hostile actions against Germany."

In January 1943, mainly to support Jewish refugees from Poland and Slovakia, an aid committee was set up by Zionists in Budapest under the name Vaadah.* One of its leaders was Rezsö Kastner. Joel Brand, another member of the committee, worked on smuggling persecuted Jews from Poland to Hungary, which then was not so hard-hit. The refugees arrived empty-handed and were furnished by the committee with food, clothing, shelter and false identification papers.

When the occupation took place and the Germans attacked the Hungarian Jews, Kastner and Brand

* Vaadah Ezra va Hazalah

contacted Eichmann regarding ransoming those being deported. Kastner traveled to Switzerland often to meet representatives of the American War Refugee Board and the Jewish organizations there in the hope of getting the required sums. Kastner had many negotiating sessions with Eichmann and his henchmen. The Germans came back with steadily rising demands for larger and larger amounts, while no sure guarantee was given in return that the deportations would stop.

On one occasion, they promised to stop the deportations for the sum of two million dollars, which those on the Jewish side succeeded with great difficulty in getting together. Yet when the money was collected, the matter appeared in a different light, since Eichmann changed his mind again because of an order from Himmler and now demanded a completely different compensation for stopping the transportation to Auschwitz. This was the well-known German proposal to release a million Jews for a commitment from the British-American side to deliver 10,000 trucks — one for every hundred Jews — to the German armed forces. To show that he was in earnest, Eichmann promised Kastner a "test shipment" of Jews to Switzerland at a fixed price of one thousand dollars a head. The promise was kept, and in two phases around 3,000 Jews were sent to Switzerland, some of them from the concentration camp Bergen-Belsen in western Germany.

To negotiate the matter of the trucks with the western allies, Brand was sent to Turkey, from which he proceeded to Syrian Palestine. However, he was arrested and held there by the British Secret Service, destroying the whole mission.*

For the Allies, it was unthinkable to agree to any arrangement that would strengthen the German war potential. An assurance from the German negotiators that the trucks would only be used on the eastern front was of course regarded as an attempt to drive a wedge between the Russians and the other Allies.

Winning the war as quickly as possible was the important thing. In this context, the lives of a million Jews became secondary in importance to the Allies. A contributing, but obviously not decisive reason that the plan failed may also have been the question of how it could be carried out in practicality. How could the transport of one million persons take place in the midst of a raging war? Which countries would be willing to accept them?

True, in Hungary we could see that a certain emigration to Palestine, by those Jews who had succeeded in obtaining the so-called Palestine certificates, had already taken place. But the English had been very restrictive when it came to issuing such certificates, and after the German occupation this traffic ceased altogether.

It did seem as though the Allies looked on the mass emigration of Jews from Nazi-occupied Europe with a certain uneasiness. At negotiations between the Jewish representative in Istanbul and the British authorities concerning Brand's proposal, one of the Englishmen is said to have exclaimed: "But where in all the world shall we send them?"

* A detailed description of the course of these events is to be found in Alex Weissberg's book, *Desperate Mission*.

Many stories are told, too, of the first years of the war, when the Germans allowed a certain emigration of Jews — how the fully loaded ships had to go from port to port without being accepted.

There has been speculation about the Germans' motives for their various offers to release a large number of Jews in return for cash or trucks, contributions that could hardly have affected their war effort decisively. Could this calculation have motivated them: with an eye on some day of reckoning, to make the Allies seem to have been accessories to the crime; to be able to show that the outside world had never been willing to open its doors to the victims of Nazism?

It was in this situation that hopes turned to what the neutral countries, chiefly Sweden and Switzerland, could do to aid the Jewish population *in situ*.

It has sometimes been said that the Germans' truck proposition to the Americans and British contributed to increasing the Russians' mistrust of all efforts to rescue the Jews and specifically affected their later attitude toward Wallenberg.

Note, in this connection, the Russians' total indifference to the fate of the Jews. Even though, for the reasons given above, the Americans and English could not agree to Eichmann's proposal, they could have let Brand return home, there to use delaying tactics in stalling further deportations to Auschwitz. Recognized spokesmen for that action included the American War Refugee Board which, as will later be described, came to play a decisive role in the financing of Wallenberg's operation.

But continued contact with Eichmann was rendered impossible by Russian veto. Deputy foreign minister Vishinsky, in June 1944, informed the American embassy in Moscow that the Soviet government regarded as undesirable the conduct of any negotiation whatsoever with the Germans on the Jewish question.

This was the same Vishinsky, who, in a note to the Swedish government on August 18, 1947, denied that Wallenberg was in the Soviet Union!

Another attempt of the War Refugee Board to rescue the Hungarian Jews was a proposal submitted by the Board's representative in Bern, McClelland, to the Allies, to bomb the railroad connections from Hungary to Auschwitz and also the gas chambers themselves, so as to halt the deportations. The proposal was turned down with the justification that it was not practical at a time when all available aircraft were needed for directly war-related operations. But in this case, too, the Russians' negative attitude may have been behind the refusal.*

The new Jewish ordinances, introduced in the spring of 1944, were a sinister omen of things to come. Step by step, the Jewish population of Hungary was robbed of all its civil rights. Jews were required to wear a yellow star on the breast, and failure to do this was punished with imprisonment or death.

I will never forget the day the ordinances went into effect. One could see Budapest's Jews, that is, every third and fourth person one met, marked with the yellow star as a sign that they belonged to a despised

* A more detailed description of the Soviets' attitude may be found in Arthur Morse's book, *While Six Million Died* and Henry L. Feingold's *The Politics of Rescue*.

pariah class that had been doomed to destruction. Against the dark clothing most of them wore, the six-pointed stars of a poisonous cadmium yellow felt seemed luminous. Some bore them with the resignation of a thousand years of suffering, others were too proud to show themselves outdoors with this mark on their breasts. Some tried pathetically to hide their stars momentarily with briefcase, package or purse, as one hides a handicap. Of course this, too, was punishable. German soldiers checked that the ordinances were obeyed, but the Hungarian Arrow Crossmen, who willingly informed on those they knew, were even more dangerous.

The property of the Jews was seized and they were not allowed to practice any profession. They were forbidden to visit restaurants or theaters. They could not sit on park benches, nor were they allowed to travel by train or car. Later, they were concentrated in special camps or buildings, marked with the yellow star, and were not allowed to show themselves outdoors. Their suffering mounted in a daily *crescendo furioso*. In the end, ghettos were set up, the last stage before deportation to the gas chambers in Auschwitz or Birkenau.

One asks why the Jews did not resist their executioners at an earlier stage? Even the Warsaw ghetto's heroic but hopeless struggle against superior odds first took place after almost a half million Jews had been massacred and only 60,000 remained. One explanation may be that a large number of the Jewish people, in the beginning, regarded the stories about the killing in the gas chambers as exaggerated. Experience had prepared them for being beaten and tortured, but even German Nazis could hardly be so bestial as to intend to stamp out a whole people. Many had received letters from relatives in German concentration camps which spoke of good, humane treatment. They fancied that, for men, it was simply a matter of forced làbor, and for women and children, a temporary sojourn in camps, until the family could be reunited after the war.

In this connection, the Germans cleverly utilized the especially established Jewish Councils for their purposes. These "representatives" of the Jewish establishment were indoctrinated by the Germans and persuaded that no evil would befall the Jews as long as they remained calm. Therefore, under the Jewish Councils' direction, the concentration of the Jews into ghettos went rather smoothly, all in all. There, however, the Jews became isolated from the outside world and family members were separated from one another. The treatment then aimed to bring them to a state of total physical and psychic exhaustion, sickness and death. Thus the Nazis had no trouble transporting the survivors — who by then were too weak to resist — to the gas chambers.

On one occasion, the legation received through the Foreign Office an appeal for help from a Swedish woman who had formerly been married to a Hungarian Jew and who wanted us to try to rescue their ten-year-old son, Ragnar. The boy was living with his paternal grandparents in Pécs in southern Hungary, since his father had been drafted into forced labor. At first, we saw no possibility of intervening. Pécs lies about a hundred and twenty miles from Budapest and the mission had had discouraging results from earlier attempts to save persons living in the countryside. However, I received the assignment to see what could be done and early one morning drove out to Pécs. Happily, the Nazis and their elimination of Jews from the countryside had not yet reached this place. Of course the Jews could only live in certain sections and they all wore the yellow star, but there had not yet been any deportations from Pécs.

After much searching, I succeeded in finding Ragnar. There was a great commotion among his Jewish relatives, and his old grandmother refused to let him be taken from her. I explained that his father should be allowed to decide this question, and so we all went out to the internment camp on the outskirts where he was working.

He realized that this was a chance of rescue for his son and immediately gave his permission. Then, with great emotion, he parted from his son. After a farewell meal with Ragnar's relatives, I put the boy in the legation car, took the yellow star from his chest, and returned with him to Budapest.

Ragnar lived with us for a while and then was sent by plane to Stockholm, where he was happily reunited with his mother. Later I learned that the day after my visit, all the Jews in Pécs had been shut up in a ghetto and were shortly thereafter deported to Poland.

During the spring and summer, practically all the Jews in the countryside were gradually eliminated.*

* According to what later came out during the Eichmann trial, and was confirmed in a conversation I had with the prosecutor of the trial during a visit to Jerusalem a year or so ago, about 600,000 Jews were deported from Hungary during the period May 15 to July 7. Most often, the frequency reached four trains a day containing a total of 12,000 persons.

Eyewitnesses who visited the legation gave us terrifying descriptions of how various parts of Hungary were "cleansed" of Jews. Then came the turn of the Budapest suburbs. When I heard that a large number of Jews from the suburbs — I was told around 15,000 — had been taken to a brickyard outside the city, I went there to see it with my own eyes.

Within the brickyard, which had an area about the same as Norrmalms Square in Stockholm, thousands of Jews stood or lay tightly packed together. They had been kept there for nearly a week without food or drink and without shelter from weather or wind. It was a terrible sight.

The area was fenced in and guarded by Hungarian gendarmes equipped with submachine guns. The Hungarian gendarmes, as distinguished from both the army (Honved) and the regular city police, were known for their extreme anti-Semitism and their ruthlessness. They therefore became the Germans' willing tools against the Jews.

Around this arena stood the inhabitants of the district, as silent, frightened spectators. A German SS officer, a specialist in Jewish matters and equipped with a long whip, served as "adviser." While I stood there, a train with empty cattle cars was shifted onto a spur that served the brickyard. The doors were opened, and as many Jews as possible — men, women and children — were forced into the cars with kicks and blows. Eighty or so persons were stuffed into each car, which would normally accommodate half so many. A mother tried to hide her child and prevent its being taken along. A soldier saw this, grasped the child by the leg and flung it into the wagon.

As a kind of humanitarian gesture, a bucket of water was placed in each wagon, then the doors were closed up and nailed shut with boards. Then the train is said to have steamed around Hungary a week or so, during which time many died or went insane. Those who survived got to continue their journey to the gas chambers in Poland.

Because the deportations during May and June grew more and more inclusive, and proceeded in more and more inhuman forms, on June 30, 1944, King Gustav V of Sweden sent the following plea to Horthy: "Having received word of the extraordinarily harsh methods your government has applied against the Jewish population of Hungary, I permit myself to turn to your Highness personally, to beg in the name of humanity that you take measures to save those who still remain to be saved of this unfortunate people. This plea has been evoked by my long-standing feelings of friendship for your country and my sincere concern for Hungary's good name and reputation in the community of nations."

I was with Danielsson when he delivered this message to Horthy. It was pathetic to hear the old regent's assurance that no Hungarian authorities could even imagine collaborating in these crimes.

Of course Horthy was, like the rest of the Hungarian aristocracy and other large groups of the Hungarian people, known for not having any warm feelings for the Jews. Yet he disassociated himself sharply from the barbarian methods used by the Germans, as would be seen later.

However, the Hungarians, too, had been guilty of serious excesses. It is known that, in 1941, 12,000

Jews were deported from eastern Hungary to the German-administered Ukraine, on the pretext that the Jews were not Hungarian citizens. The Hungarians could hardly have been ignorant of the fate that awaited these Jews as soon as they fell into German hands.

Another Hungarian outrage occurred in January 1942, at Báscka in the area taken from Yugoslavia, when about 4,000 Serbian Jews were massacred, thanks to the exertions of the local Hungarian authorities.

When the then prime minister, the extremely anti-Semitic Bardossy, was succeeded by the more moderate Kállay, one of Kállay's first assignments was to bring to justice those responsible for this violence against the Jews. This trial subsequently contributed to the further deterioration of relations between Budapest and Berlin.

To understand the attitude of the Hungarian people toward the Jewish question, perhaps it is appropriate here to mention something of the recent history of the Jews in Hungary.

Ever since the beginning of the century the Jews had, through ability and industry, come to play an important role in Hungarian social life, not only in the world of business (which not only the Hungarian landowning classes but even the farmers had always looked down on) but even in the independent professions. Before the outbreak of the First World War, Jews constituted more than half of Budapest's approximately three thousand lawyers. The medical profession had a similar percentage. Also, the key positions in cultural life — the press, publishing, film and theater — were often occupied by Jews. Besides this, about a fourth of Hungary's land area was owned by Jews.

This development in the direction of increasing Jewish influence had not been regarded as any problem. On the contrary, those in power acknowledged that, to a large extent, they had the Jews to thank for Hungary's economic and cultural welfare. Besides this, the Jews posed no important national threat because they were assimilating with the Hungarians at an increasing rate.

When Hungary was partitioned after the First World War, however, the situation changed. The notorious Jewish Communist, Béla Kun, seized power in 1919 after an uprising. The Communists were soon defeated, though, by a counterrevolution led by Horthy, then an admiral. The governments that followed had a clearly anti-Semitic attitude. Neither was the situation improved by the flight of thousands of Jews into central Hungary from the ceded areas in Slovakia and Transylvania. These added an unwelcome surplus to an already abundant unemployment. For those Hungarian landowners who had lost their properties in the ceded areas and now went out into the labor market, the newly arrived Jews became unwished-for competitors.

Thus the wave of anti-Semitism that followed had hardly anything in common with the Nazi racial doctrines but had a more sociopolitical character. Yet a foundation had been laid for the actions of the Hungarian Nazis that were about to take place.

On July 12, the following reply came from Horthy to the Swedish king's plea: "I have received the telegraphic appeal sent me by your Majesty. With feelings of the deepest understanding, I ask your Majesty to be persuaded that I am doing everything that, in the present situation, lies in my power to assure that the principles of humanity and justice are respected. I esteem to a high degree the feelings of friendship for my country which animate your Majesty and I ask that your Majesty preserve these feelings toward the Hungarian people in these times of severe trial."

It is said that, after the Swedish king's intervention, Horthy stepped in and succeeded, for the time being, in preventing any further deportations from the capital. The Christian churches and the International Red Cross, too, protested, and the American secretary of state, Cordell Hull, sent through the Swiss legation a warning of serious retaliation against Hungary, should the deportations not be stopped. Yet no one believed that, in the long run, Veesenmayer would go along with sparing the Jews of Budapest.

Now a difficult and trying time began for the legation and its members. We were besieged by Jews who suspected what was coming and pleaded for help. Supplicants jammed the reception room, and the queue snaked a long way down the street.

However, our ability to help all of them was limited. From a strict juridical standpoint, we could only intervene on behalf of Swedish citizens and citizens of those countries whose interests, because of the war, Sweden represented in Hungary. Yet something had to be done, and quickly. Every day the situation of the Jews worsened. In the beginning, we issued provisional Swedish passports — really a kind of travel document, which under certain circumstances could be given even to non-citizens of Sweden, that is, persons with especially close connections to Sweden through family relationship or business connections. The provisional passports at first gave no great protection, but the legation gradually succeeded through negotiations with the Hungarian authorities in winning the concession that the holders of such passes would be treated as Swedish citizens and be released from the requirement of wearing the yellow star. In this way, as a rule, they could avoid internment and deportation. To make sure that the value of these passports was not diminished by inflation, we were obliged to limit their number. This made it necessary to find other solutions, and our inventiveness was sorely tested. For a large number of the Jews, the application for Swedish citizenship had been made through Swedish relatives in Sweden, and for these Jews we issued certificates which read something like this:

"It is hereby certified that the *Swedish* relatives, domiciled in Sweden, of John Doe, have on his behalf applied to the appropriate authorities for Swedish citizenship, upon which a decision may shortly be expected. For this reason, the Legation calls upon all authorities, both civil and military, in any action concerning John Doe, to take due consideration of the matter cited above."

The certificate was decked out with the Minister's signature, stamps and seal, the whole panoply of authority.

However, a decree was soon issued to the effect that Hungary did not recognize any foreign citizenship that was conferred after the 19th of March, 1944, that is to say, the day of the German invasion. We then went over to fabricating similar certificates for those Jews who had been granted visas for travel to Sweden. The worth of these certificates, which became the forerunners of the so-called protective passports issued during Wallenberg's time, was perhaps at first sight debatable. There probably were few who held these certificates who allowed themselves any hope of escaping from Hungary with their aid. However, the chief intention was simply to gain time. We were encouraged in our continued exertions by reports from persons who got safely through raids and house searches by showing such documents to the usually uneducated and not overly intelligent Nazi functionaries.

In a rather short time, the legation had issued no less than 700 provisional passports and certificates. The rumor of our work spread and the host of supplicants swelled day by day.

The whole Swedish mission — the minister, the Swedish academic and Red Cross representative in Budapest, Waldemar Langlet, the consular officer, Dénes von Mezey, the typists, Birgit Brulin and Margareta Bauer, as well as I myself — worked day and night during these months. When it became clear that our strength would be insufficient for this new enterprise, the minister approached our Ministry of Foreign Affairs about reinforcing the legation staff.

The Arrival of Raoul Wallenberg

Danielsson's request for more personnel happened to coincide with the negotiations that were going on in Stockholm between the Foreign Office and representatives of the American War Refugee Board, the World Jewish Congress, and the United States' minister in Stockholm, Herschel Johnson, concerning the dispatch of a Swede to Hungary to head a rescue effort for the Jews.

The negotiations led to Raoul Wallenberg receiving the assignment, and he was appointed Secretary of Legation in the Budapest mission.

Wallenberg was 32 years of age and belonged to the well-known Wallenberg family of financiers. His father, who was a naval officer, died just before he was born, and his mother was later remarried to Fredrik von Dardel. Raoul Wallenberg had originally been educated as an architect and then had shifted over to a business career. Both my wife and I had known Raoul for a long time, and our friendship had been confirmed during the last few years when, as representative for a Swedish company — the Central European Trading Company — he had visited Hungary on various occasions.

I was convinced that no one was better qualified for the assignment than Wallenberg. He was a clever negotiator and organizer, unconventional, extraordinarily inventive and cool-headed, and something of a

49

go-getter. Besides this, he was very good at languages and well grounded in Hungarian affairs. At heart, he was a great idealist and a warm human being.

Wallenberg arrived at the legation on the 9th of July, 1944, equipped rather oddly for a diplomat. He was carrying two knapsacks, a sleeping bag, a windbreaker, and a revolver. But this equipment would be put to good use in the months ahead. "The revolver is just to give me courage," he said to me in his typically joking way. "I hope I'll never have to use it. But now I'm in a hurry to get to work. I've read your reports, but could you bring me up to date?"

I related that the deportations from the countryside had been brought to an end and that the major part of Budapest's Jews had not yet been affected. The deportation of these Jews seemed to have been postponed, in accordance with the appeal by the Swedish king. "But everything depends on what the Germans have in mind," I added. "It's hardly believable that they will go along with sparing the Jews of the capital for good."

"What documents have you issued the Jews?" Wallenberg asked.

I showed him the provisional passports, the visa certificates and the Red Cross protection letters. Wallenberg looked at the documents and said, after a pause: "I think I've got an idea for a new and maybe more effective document."

In this way, the idea of the so-called protective passports was born at our first meeting. These were the identification papers in blue and yellow with the three crowns emblem on them that would come to be the saving of tens of thousands of Jews.

As soon as he arrived, Wallenberg organized the continued rescue operation, under the direction of the <u>chief of</u> mission. This operation came to be financed mainly by the War Refugee Board in Washington which, through the American legation in Stockholm, placed substantial sums at Wallenberg's disposal. But large sums also flowed in from voluntary donations inside Hungary.

A special department was created, with Wallenberg as head and mostly volunteer Jewish manpower as its personnel. By this means, the other members of the mission could gain some badly needed relief from such matters. For my own part, I could now take up some long-neglected duties, such as preparing plans for the possible evacuation of our mission from Budapest to the countryside, putting the air-raid shelter in order, storing supplies, and so on.

51

Visit to Stockholm

In August 1944 I traveled home with my family to leave them in Stockholm. I also had Danielsson's sanction for requesting further reinforcement of our mission. I took back with me attaché Lars Berg, who had already smelled powder during his service in Department B of the Berlin legation, consular officer Göte Carlsson, and Red Cross representative Asta Nilsson, who had experience of earlier aid work in Hungary.

"True, she's no man," said Baron Stjernstedt of the Red Cross to me on my departure — somewhat apologetically, thinking of the conditions, unsuitable for ladies, that Hungary now faced. "However," he added, "when it really matters, she's better than most men." Events would prove that this was no exaggeration.

While in Stockholm, I also met with Iver Olsen and Francis Cunningham of the American legation, who worked on getting help to the Hungarian Jews, among other things, and also kept in touch with Ullein-Reviczky. They expressed their great admiration for the contributions of our Swedish legation in Budapest. Olsen, who represented the War Refugee Board, confirmed that there would be no problem in continuously putting funds at the disposal of the activities Wallenberg had just begun.

Ullein-Reviczky, who had continued to keep close contact with the Allied missions in Stockholm after his

52

resignation as Hungarian minister to Stockholm, expressed great distress over developments in his homeland. True, Kállay had started off on the right track, he thought. His firm stance with the Germans and more humane treatment of the Jews had been appreciated by the western Allies. However, this good will had been demolished at once when the Hungarians had allowed themselves to be occupied by the Germans without resistance or even very much protest. The only possibility for Hungary to receive friendly treatment at the peace settlement, now fast approaching after the German defeats, was for Horthy himself to take over the responsibility of governing. He ought to depose Sztójay with the help of the Hungarian military and himself set up a military regime. Then he should let the Allies know, through the neutral legations in Budapest, that he was willing to make peace and ask their help against Germany.

"This," Ullein-Reviczky continued, "is Hungary's last chance. If we continue to run the Germans' errands, then we are really lost." I could not help but be touched by his words. His patriotism burned as brightly as in those conversations we had had earlier, when he was press chief in Budapest. He concluded with the question of whether I would be willing to do him and Hungary a favor. "What is that?" I asked.

"What I've just told you, I have written in a personal letter to my personal friend, Horthy's son Miklós, and asked him to persuade his father to do as I have proposed. Would you be willing to take the letter with you now, when you return to Hungary?"

And that I did, with the approval of our Foreign Office.

As will later be seen in the chapter called "A New Government," Horthy took Ullein-Reviczky's advice and deposed Sztójay. Yet he did not have enough strength to go the whole way and break with the Germans. Thereby, they won time for their counter-move: the Arrow Cross revolution.

During my short visit to Stockholm, the news arrived that Russian troops had occupied Rumania in just one day and already stood at the Hungarian border.

I advanced my return trip to be back in time. But the Russian conquest of Hungary did not go as quickly as I thought it would.

The New Organization of the Legation

After his arrival in Budapest, Berg, with Carlsson's assistance, took over the legation's Department B, that is, the department that looked after the interests of various other powers.

Sweden was at that time looking after the interests in Hungary of no less than seven nations, the Soviet Union among them. Asta Nilsson, in collaboration with Langlet, who was responsible for the Red Cross' other activities, went right to work organizing assistance to Hungarian children.

Unfortunately, later in their collaboration Asta Nilsson and Langlet clashed. Because they were both Red Cross representatives, a dualism arose and Asta Nilsson refused to take orders from Langlet. The problem was solved by having them both report directly to the mission, who did their best to coordinate their activities. Both, each on his own, made highly valued contributions. In principle, the Red Cross' work was to assist all those suffering from the war, regardless of race or nationality, but naturally enough this aid chiefly came to concern the Jews in their precarious situation.

Langlet, with the help of his wife, Nina, carried out his work dauntlessly. He had room in his great heart for everyone, and there was no limit to the number of Red Cross protection letters he personally made out and signed. The number of locations, among them convents and hospitals, that were placed under the protection of the Red Cross increased by the day. Later, it would prove more and more difficult to protect these from the Nazis. In the legation, we were justifiedly worried about Langlet's activities and it became almost impossible, in the prevailing situation, to keep track of or gain any overview of these activities. In his book, *Verk och dagar i Budapest* ("Works and Days in Budapest"), Langlet describes his situation thus:

"Gradually our work had reached such a scope that those seeking help streamed to us by the thousands, and the domestic Red Cross, which was subject to the Ministry of War, at last was obliged to bid us begone, before the whole thing ended in disaster. No harm was really done by this, rather the opposite. We chose some of the places they offered us, and there we could set ourselves up as we pleased. Soon we had laid claim to a dozen or so houses or apartments in various sections of the city, for use as our offices, besides our already numerous established or intended shelters.

"People began jokingly to call us the city's biggest landlord, and our envoy, who was worried about what he called 'an inflation of locations,' made greater and greater difficulties when I asked his signature on the document we displayed to show that the premises were under official protection. However, most of the time I got my wishes more or less granted by never saying no, for my part, when he asked us to handle those who were swamping him with impossible demands for a hiding place within the legation."

To round out the picture of the Swedish operation at this time, it should be mentioned that still one more

Swede was attached to the mission, that is, Consul Yngve Ekmark. He was the Swedish Match Company's director in Zagreb, who was at times in Budapest. Among his other assignments, Ekmark was asked to organize a special unit for purchasing, distributing and storing food, medicine and clothing for our aid activities. The assignment grew considerably larger and more difficult than we had expected in the beginning, and his experience and practical knowledge found useful application. Unfortunately, the greater part of the purchased food was lost when the Arrow Crossmen plundered the legation in December. Through November, though, significant quantities had been distributed to those in need.

Thus, adding Wallenberg's department to those operations, a comprehensive organization had come into being in a relatively short time. The responsibility of coordinating and otherwise holding together this organization became the minister's and my most important assignment.

Wallenberg's operation had meanwhile been gradually extended. A number of offices had been set up in various parts of the city, and his staff now numbered around 400 persons.

Wallenberg succeeded in gaining the agreement of the Hungarian authorities that the Jews on his staff should be freed from wearing the yellow star, and this gave them greater protection and freedom of movement. In his department, the protective passports mentioned earlier were issued. They were furnished with the minister's signature and explained straightforwardly that the holder and his property were under the protection of the Swedish legation until such time as his emigration to Sweden could be arranged. That is, the Swedish government had declared itself willing to accept all those Jews who were provided with protective passports. But all attempts to transport these Jews to Sweden ran aground, in the end, on the impossibility of obtaining permission for passage through Germany.

For the Hungarian government's part, it was promised that holders of our protective passports would not be deported. They were allowed to live in certain buildings in Pest rented by the legation, the so-called "Swedish houses," while awaiting their "emigration" to Sweden. The number of protective passports approved by the Hungarian authorities rose to five thousand. Later on, more and more Jews were spirited into these buildings in secrecy, without the authorities' permission. Soon the total number of Jews under Swedish protection rose to more than twice the number authorized, or from 15 to 20,000. Add to this the great throng of Jews, both adults and children, who were hidden or otherwise helped through the efforts of Langlet and Asta Nilsson.

Other foreign legations, too, the Swiss, Spanish, Portuguese, and the Papal Nuncio, got to work issuing identification papers of a similar sort. Ever since the German occupation began, the nuncio, Angelo Rotta, had been making energetic representations to the Hungarian government to help the Jews. Rotta's actions were in stark contrast to the passivity shown by his chief, Pope Pius XII. During the persecution of the Jews in Italy, his silence was notable. As regards Hungary, Rotta had to work alone, without any particular support from the Vatican.

58

At the Swiss legation, Consul Charles Lutz carried on a tireless labor in the Jews' behalf. Once the Swiss had assumed the British interests in Hungary, they took care of conveying certificates to those Jews who had been granted entry to Palestine. True, this emigration had, as mentioned earlier, stopped altogether with the German occupation. However, this did not hinder Lutz from issuing papers or protective passports for a large number of fictional or actual holders of such certificates. The number approved by the Hungarian authorities rose to around 8,000, but in actuality the Swiss followed our example and took considerably more under their protection.

It is also well known how the Swiss, by taking over the interests in Hungary of San Salvador at American request, succeeded in furnishing several thousand Jews with papers of citizenship in that Central American country. Actually, San Salvador had no citizens in Hungary, as the Americans were well aware. But what was involved was continually trying to find new ways to save human lives, and the Swiss, after long negotiation, succeeded in getting the Hungarian ministry to approve the "citizens of San Salvador."

In consultation with Wallenberg's department, the authorities arranged for a further number of dwellings to be placed at the disposal of Jews holding documents issued by the other foreign missions. Under Swedish leadership, the provision of the "foreign houses" with food was organized, and special hospitals were set up. After the war was over, it was shown that the total number of Jews who were thus rescued directly by the foreign legations and the International Red Cross amounted to nearly 50,000, of which almost half were saved by Swedish efforts, chiefly Wallenberg's.

During the summer, trying to get the deportations going again, the head of the Hungarian gendarmes, Lt. Col. Ferenczy, together with Baky and Endre, planned a coup to depose Horthy. The plans were supported by Eichmann, who had found the regent's presence altogether too uncomfortable.

On the pretext that they had to keep order in the capital, large forces of gendarmes concentrated in Budapest early in July, intending to overthrow Horthy. However, the regent had received word of the plan. He had time to call in several armored and infantry units and, with their help, he ordered the gendarmes to disperse.

Thereafter, the power wielded by Baky and Endre was considerably curtailed. Horthy's firmness was praised, and Budapest's Jews felt they might look forward to better days.

A New Government In Hungary

At the end of 1944, Rumania surrendered and it was only a question of time before the Russians would pour across Hungary's borders. Horthy, who had for some time contemplated deposing Sztójay, now seized the chance and replaced his government with a military government under General Lakatos. The Germans were presented with a *fait accompli* and in this militarily critical situation they held back. Horthy apparently didn't intend to break with the Germans, anyway. Even if putting in a new government seemed to be part of preparations for Hungarian capitulation, Horthy was still unwilling to open the borders to the Soviet armies. Evidently he still hoped to be able to stop the Russians till the western Allies could occupy Hungary.

After the Sztójay government had been deposed, the situation of the Jews improved. The Germans agreed to let the Hungarians handle the Jewish question themselves. The bloodhounds Endre and Baky were fired, and Eichmann left Hungary.

The deportations stopped, and the Jews were gradually to be released from the internment camps. In Wallenberg's department, they could draw breath, and Wallenberg himself expected that the department could soon be shut down. He planned to return to Sweden, having completed his assignment.

But the Jews of Budapest had only gained a momentary reprieve, and instead of closing down,

Situa's interminable

Wallenberg and his department would now face new and considerably more difficult problems than before.

In the beginning of 1944, Finland broke off relations with Hungary, after having taken herself out of the war, and arranged a cease-fire with the Soviet Union. When we assumed the Finnish interests in Hungary, I received the assignment of organizing the journey home for the Finnish mission. It was our proposal that an official from the Protocol Department accompany the mission on their journey. Those in charge at Protocol picked up the cue. Here was a golden opportunity for someone to "jump ship" in Sweden. A young government official, Andor Eszterházy, got the chance.

Everything went as planned all the way to the German-Danish border. The Finns were allowed to pass, but our Hungarian friend was stopped by the Germans, giving as their reason that an Arrow Cross revolution had broken out in Hungary and they had received orders to send him back. Thus our plan was ignominiously thwarted.

The Arrow Crossmen Take Over

On October 15, 1944, the arrow crossmen, with German help, staged a coup and deposed the Lakatos government. It was the same day the legation had arranged for the last of the Swedish women and children in Hungary to travel home to Sweden. I was at the railroad station in Budapest with Berg and Carlsson, and we had just installed the Swedes in a railroad car reserved for them when, suddenly, a loudspeaker announced that Hungary had entered into a cease-fire with Russia. Therefore, all Hungarians were urged to lay down their arms and to show their solidarity with the government.

This announcement caused great confusion at the station. Since I had the responsibility for the transportation of the Swedes, I was at first rather ambivalent about whether it was practical, under such conditions, to let them proceed, especially since the Swedish car was a part of a German troop train. If the announcement were true, it was probable that the train would be shot at en route or sabotaged by the Hungarians. There was no time for deliberation, for the train was on the point of leaving for Vienna.

The reaction among the German soldiers was sharp. They felt embittered by the Hungarian government's treachery, which came like a stab in the back just when the situation on the eastern front had begun to be critical. The Germans did not look especially kindly upon the group of Swedish civilians who were taking up room meant for soldiers. With our combined strength, Berg, Carlsson and I succeeded in stopping some German soldiers who tried to evict the Swedes by force. The soldiers reported us to the German transport officer, who came up red-faced with anger and declared in a loud voice that the Swedish group had to leave the train to make room for the soldiers. I answered in an equally loud voice that we had no intention of taking orders from him. If he had any wishes he could forward them to the German minister, Veesenmayer, with whom our legation maintained the customary diplomatic relations. That did it. The officer obviously hesitated a bit when he heard the dreaded name of Veesenmayer and reluctantly agreed to the Swedes keeping their places on the train. But he declared that I would have to take the responsibility if anything happened to the Swedes enroute. "You're going to be under fire, you'll see!" ("Sie werden sehen, es wird geschossen!"), he said to several of the frightened Swedes. However, I felt that the situation in Budapest would, in all probability, be worse and the risks for the Swedes greater if they should stay. So I gave the order for departure.

Some days later, to our relief, we received a message that the train had arrived in Germany without incident and that the Swedish group, in good condition, had continued their trip to Sweden.

On the way home from the station, we found the streets blocked by German military. Hungarian Nazis, mostly rabble, who had been armed to the teeth by the Germans, were everywhere. Raids, ransackings and arrests followed in quick succession.

This is what had happened: The Hungarian regent, together with a few faithful followers, had long planned Hungary's withdrawal from the war on an agreed day. Through their spies, the Germans had got word of this. To make Horthy show his hand, the assassination of his son Miklós was arranged. In the attempt, Horthy's adjutants, two Hungarian officers, were shot down and Miklós wounded. Horthy then decided to undertake the coup the same day and sent his chief of staff to the radio station with orders to read a message from the regent that the war was over, for Hungary's part. The Germans, who were prepared for that, reacted at once. The radio station was occupied by German military and after an hour a new message was broadcast to the Hungarian people, in which the regent's message was said to have been a mistake and that they should continue their fight against the Russians. The German who was given the assignment to lead the operation against Horthy was the well-known Colonel Otto Skorzeny, who had earlier freed Mussolini from the mountain fortress Gran Sasso.

Thereupon, the German minister, Veesenmayer, went to the Castle and explained to Horthy that he was under German "protection." To lend further emphasis to his words, Veesnmayer pointed out the window at two German tanks that had been placed outside on the lawn with their guns directed at the Castle.

Horthy gave in to superior force. He was forced to resign and to name Arrow Cross leader Ferenc Szálasi the new head of government, in return for the promise of asylum for himself and his family in Germany, as well as reunion there with his son, Miklós. The family was taken away and subsequently held prisoner in Hirschberg castle in Bayern, where they were freed by American troops at the war's end. Concerning Miklós, however, the Germans did not keep their promise. When his wounds had healed, he was put in concentration camps, first in Mauthausen and then in Dachau, where the Americans found him.

The arrow crossmen now occupied all public buildings, and Horthy's followers offered only feeble resistance. Only his elite guard took up the struggle, at the Castle. During the night, the city echoed with shots as the Hungarian guards fought against superior forces. On the morning of October 11, all resistance had been crushed.

In the foreign ministry, many of our friends were arrested. Some succeeded in going underground. They had all been betrayed by a female secretary, Baroness Zech, who had long been a member of Arrow Cross in secret and had collected detailed information about which of the officials opposed Szálasi. She now became the evil genius of the foreign ministry, with broad powers.

During the days that followed, things looked blacker than ever for the legation's continued assistance effort for the Jews. The city's street were blocked, all traffic was forbidden, and everyone waited anxiously for what was coming.

Eichmann and his henchmen returned, and for Wallenberg a hectic and dangerous period now began. But he never gave up, no matter how hopeless things looked.

I remember the day he hopped on a bicycle and traveled around to his various offices to encourage and hearten his Jewish colleagues, a trip he undertook with great personal risk.

Soon the persecution of the Jews reached a pitch that defies description. At night, we could hear the shots of the arrow crossmen's submachine guns when Jews, after being robbed of everything including their clothes, were shot down naked and thrown into the Danube.

It was at this point that the so-called international ghetto came into being, as decided by the Szálasi government. Negotiations for this had already been started under the previous government by the neutral legations, negotiations in which Wallenberg played a leading role. The buildings comprising the ghetto were furnished with Jewish stars and were under the protection of the legations. Jews who had protective passports lived there. Thus the Swedish houses mentioned earlier became part of this ghetto and some thirty buildings now received Swedish protection.

Meanwhile, two Russian armies were rapidly approaching, one from the south under Marshal Tolbukhin, and one from the east under Marshal Malinovsky. Soon only the way to the west was open from Budapest. The roads to Poland were blocked, and only Austria remained possible as a destination for the continued deportation of Jews. When the railroad was taken over for military transport and the Nazis wanted to liquidate as many Jews as possible in the time remaining, they switched to a method that broke all previous records for cruelty and mercilessness.

Thousands of people were seized where they walked, where they stood. Women in high-heeled shoes and men without overcoats were driven on foot the 125-mile-long way to Hegyeshálom, at the Hungarian-Austrian border. That is how they solved the difficult transportation problem! It took over a week to walk that distance in the winter cold and snow, without food and without the possibility of resting under shelter. Unfortunately, we had no opportunity to intervene and save these people. Only if it happened by chance that one of the deported was the holder of a Swedish protective passport were there any prospects of getting him or her conveyed back to Budapest.

On one of the first days of December 1944, Wallenberg and I set out by car along the route the Jews were being marched. We passed those masses of unfortunates, more dead than alive. Ashy-faced, they staggered forward under prodding and blows from the soldiers' rifle butts. The road was edged with bodies. We had the car full of food, which we succeeded in passing out despite such help being prohibited, but it did not go very far. At Hegyeshálom we saw how those who arrived were turned over to an SS unit under Eichmann, who counted them like cattle. "Four hundred eighty-nine — check!" ("Vier-hundert-neunundachtzig — stimmt gut!"). The Hungarian officer received a receipt that said everything was in proper order.

Before that transfer took place, we succeeded in rescuing about a hundred Jews. Some of them had the Swedish protective passport. Others we got released through sheer bluff. Wallenberg would not back down. He made repeated trips, succeeding in

68

much the same way in bringing back still more to Budapest.

In collaboration with the International Red Cross, truck convoys were organized to pass out food to the deported. Further, at Wallenberg's initiative, checkpoints were set up at the roads exiting Budapest and at the border station to hinder the deportation of Jews holding the protective passport. In this way, an estimated 1,500 Jews were saved and returned to Budapest.

Now the legation staff found it harder and harder to continue its activities. Every day armed arrow crossmen burst into places that were under the legation's protection, plundering food storage and trying to carry off the personnel. We — Wallenberg, Ekmark, Berg, Mezey, Carlsson and I — remained on full alert day and night, often having to rush out en masse to try and avert an attack of the arrow crossmen. Bluff and threats were good ways of driving them off.

The following story by Carlsson is an example of such an expedition, which is right to the point.

"One night, I had a call from a very clever secretary of Wallenberg's. I've forgotten her name, but she was a brave woman. She told me her whole family had been seized by the arrow crossmen that evening and brought to one of their headquarters — I don't remember the street and district, but it lay quite a distance away, past the Margareta Bridge on the Buda side. We drove there in a Steyer auto I had then, the woman and I, and I went into the robbers' nest and got to talk to the chief. He was a man of a sort it would do you no good to shout at. Instead, I treated him

69

with great politeness, more or less on the order of 'just between us diplomats.' I continued, in my spiel, that he was such a highly placed person that he had the authority to release the Jews who had mistakenly been arrested. I remember that, at a psychologically threatening moment in our discussion, I very politely asked him for a glass of water, whereupon he brought out wine, which I praised. Gradually, he came around to agreeing to release the seven Jews in question but he said that he wanted a receipt for them, just for form's sake. My secretary — I had introduced the woman as such — typed out a receipt saying, 'On behalf of the Swedish Legation, I hereby acknowledge the receipt of 7 Jews.' ('Im Namen der schwedischen Gesandtschaft bestätige ich den Empfang von 7 Juden'), Budapest, the date, the Legation's seal, and my name below. The seven condemned persons were brought out. Their faces were thoroughly battered, they had long lacerations, they were bloody and scared. But there was no time to discuss such matters. The man began to look as though he was regretting his decision. I quickly counted 1–2–3–4–5–6–7. Fine! I stood them in a line and commanded them to 'forward, march!' We walked past the submachine-gun boys at the door. In some incomprehensible way, I succeeded in packing all seven in the car and driving away. I remember I had to drive in first gear all the way to Wallenberg's place; otherwise the car wouldn't have been able to handle the heavy load."

The legation's continuing rescue operation became a race against time. Would we be able to hold out until the Russians came? It was a question we often asked ourselves. After long and trying negotiations with the

70

Arrow Cross leadership, in which Wallenberg most often played the decisive role, we achieved a "modus vivendi" according to which those on the Hungarian side promised to respect our five thousand Swedish protective passports. The bait we held out was the prospect of Swedish recognition for the Nazi regime in Hungary through accepting a Nazi representative in Stockholm. True, Minister Danielsson had already received a message from the Foreign Office saying that the Swedish government obviously had no intention of recognizing the Szálasi regime, but we felt that for the sake of the Jews we should let the arrow crossmen keep alive their earlier illusions. The foreign minister, the fanatical and half-mad Baron Kemény, rubbed his hands together in glee at the thought that soon he would be able to appoint himself the Arrow Cross's first emissary to Stockholm. Meanwhile, the Russians were swiftly approaching the city. Kemény began to get upset over not getting the promised message about the question of recognition. Danielsson attempted to gain time through various declarations that the decision could be expected any day now, etc., but Kemény was close to losing his patience.

Thus our relations with the Hungarian government became more strained every day. The mission's refusal to come along with the Hungarian foreign ministry staff to their evacuation refuge, Szombathely, in western Hungary, was regarded as an unfriendly act. On several occasions, critical statements about the legation and its staff came from the government. At the same time, a rumor began to go around Budapest that the arrow crossmen intended to stage a riot at the neutral legations to pillage and search for Jews.

Meanwhile, one attempt to kidnap the staff and take us to Szombathely failed. We received an official invitation to take part in a boar hunt along with the head of state himself, Szálasi, and were to appear at the foreign ministry on a certain day, dressed warmly for the hunt. We suspected, however, that an invitation to a boar hunt in the middle of a war meant that mischief was brewing and so we put off as long as possible answering the invitation. When the day of the hunt came close, the military situation had worsened so much that the event was called off.

Later on, we found out through certain channels in the foreign ministry that the hunt had been arranged so that they could take us by force to Szombathely.

Arrow Crossmen Attack the Legation and the Red Cross

One night in the beginning of December, the arrow crossmen burst into the offices of the Swedish Red Cross, arrested the staff and forbade all further Red Cross activities. The legation protested vigorously at the Hungarian Foreign Ministry and asked an immediate end to the operation against the Red Cross. We declared that otherwise we would be obliged to break off relations with Hungary and return home. At the same time we fully understood that, in such an event, the Jews in the Swedish houses would be abandoned to the Nazis. We had received relatively dependable intelligence that the arrow crossmen intended to blow the houses sky-high the moment our mission left the country. Besides that, we were responsible for the score or so of Swedish citizens who had chosen to remain in Budapest, as well as the citizens of those countries whose interests we were looking after in Budapest.

Since the Russian armies were getting nearer every day, Danielsson decided, with our unanimous support, that the legation ought to avoid an open break with the Hungarian government just now, and consequently we should remain in Budapest. Instructions had been received from the Swedish Foreign Office in mid-December to the effect that the minister could decide whether the mission or some part of it should travel home or remain. We did not hesitate to stay.

Our greatest worry was Wallenberg's safety. The arrow crossmen hated him openly and intensely. He learned several times that they intended to murder him. In conversation with one of the staff of the Swedish Red Cross, Eichmann communicated his intention to have the "Jew-dog" Wallenberg shot. Eichmann's statement *could* be simply an empty threat, meant to put a scare into the legation staff, but it was not something to leave unchallenged.

Thus we sent a telegram home to the Foreign Office, asking that the legation in Berlin be instructed to take up the matter with the Germans, pointing out at the same time that theirs was the blame for the increased outrages against the Jews and against Wallenberg's Jewish staff. From an SS source we had learned that Himmler was against these excesses and set a great deal of store by Swedish-German relations.

Consequently, the Berlin legation complained of the threat against Wallenberg and asked that the SS Command in Budapest be ordered to respect mission members and other employees.

Veesenmayer's reply to the reprimand from Berlin seems to have been that Eichmann had good reason to criticize the Swedish legation's activities on the Jews' behalf, and especially those of Wallenberg, who behaved in a "far too unconventional [!] and unacceptable way." Eichmann may well have expressed the threat referred to, Veesenmayer continued, and in such a case it should not be taken literally, but more as a warning for the future.

Soon after that, the German mission left Budapest. That same day, they sent to ask to what extent we were willing to look after their interests. However, there was neither time nor means to get instructions from Stockholm concerning our compliance with that request, as we told the Germans. Upon their repeated entreaty, Danielsson decided that for the time being we would take over the keys to their building, whereby the building would be placed under Swedish protection. I received the assignment to go over to Veesenmayer and arrange the formalities. I found the Germans engaged in burning their secret files with the greatest haste and preparing for a quick evacuation of all their personnel, before the Russian ring was finally closed around Budapest.

Veesenmayer, who had not earlier displayed any warm feelings for the Swedish mission, now received me very ingratiatingly and expressed his gratitude for the Swedish assistance. Later, this action of ours came in handy and, in a situation that was critical for both the legation and its staff members, it enabled us to obtain support from the remaining SS troops against the arrow crossmen.

During this time, the Russian armies had reached the outskirts of Budapest from two directions. The only connection still remaining open was the highway to Vienna, but it was now raked with almost uninterrupted Russian artillery fire.

Feverish attempts were made to defend the city. Each one of the bridges was mined, strategic points were fortified, and tank traps and barbed-wire barriers were built in the central parts of the city. There were many indications that the Germans intended to evacuate at the last minute and turn the city's defenses over to the Hungarian troops. These were not considered to be worth much in combat, so there was hope that the city might surrender without a struggle. However, we expected there to be a transition period of a few days between the evacuation of the German troops and the entry of the Russians into the city, a period when the Nazi rabble would have a free hand! So with Danielsson's approval, I approached the Hungarian resistance movement — with whom the legation had been in touch on various earlier occasions — concerning the possibility of getting help, should the legation and its offices be subjected to the rabble's violence. They promised to put a force at our disposal. I considered that we could now face the future with something like assurance. We also obtained our own weapons and picked up on the black market a couple of Russian-made submachine guns. One of the members of the resistance and I tried the weapons out on his father's hunting preserve early one morning, with the panicked game leaping away in all directions.

The weapons gave us a feeling of safety, even though we knew they could only be used in self-defense in the most extreme situations. They were available to those on watch at the legation but luckily were never put to actual use. Events turned in a direction different from that which we anticipated.

Two days before Christmas, 1944, Wallenberg and I were summoned to the Foreign Ministry, where Acting Foreign Minister Vöczköndy received us. The foreign minister himself, like the rest of the government, had already left the city.

Vöczköndy had earlier been military attaché at the Hungarian legation in Stockholm, but because of his openly declared membership in the Arrow Cross the Swedish government had ordered him to leave the country. Since then, his feelings about Sweden were, to put it mildly, cool, and during the autumn he had done everything he could to hinder and counter the legation's work.

Within the ministry, great haste was visible, since they evidently were preparing an eleventh-hour evacuation of the remaining personnel. Vöczköndy explained that the Hungarian government, which for the present found itself situated in the city of Sopron in western Hungary, had decided that all those agencies still stationed in Budapest, including the Swedish mission, should be evacuated that very evening because of the suddenly deteriorated military situation. I responded that the legation could not agree to that. We had decided to remain. Besides, it was impossible to arrange the mission's evacuation on such short notice. Vöczköndy rejoined scornfully that the Swedish Ministry of Foreign Affairs had given him a respite of only two hours to leave the Hungarian legation in Stockholm. We would have to accept the same treatment. Should we refuse, he could take no responsibility for the consequences. To my question of whether by that he meant violence against the mission, I received only evasive replies.

I then returned at once to the legation to warn the others. They should not remain at the legation during the next twenty-four hours and should preferably not spend the night in their usual lodgings. I was not at all sure what might happen. To the very last, we refused to believe that an attack on the legation itself and a violation of its extraterritoriality would be mounted by Hungarian officials acting in their official capacity. However, for safety's sake, I sent a code telegram to the Foreign Office immediately, describing what had happened. This turned out to be the legation's last message to the outside world.

At five a.m. on the morning of the 24th, I was awakened by a telephone call from Margareta Bauer who said in her calm, laconic Scandian, "Here they come!" She told me that a group of about 50 arrow crossmen, armed with submachine guns, had driven up to the legation in a bus and were now forcing their way into our building, into Department B of the Finnish legation, and into the house beside the legation where she and Asta Nilsson lived. It was clear that their intention was to carry off the staff forcibly. I told her to delay the departure as long as she could, so that meanwhile I would have time to intervene with the help of the German and Hungarian military authorities. At the same time, I called up Department B, where Berg answered. He said that the arrow crossmen had just burst in and told him that he would have to come along in the transportation they had arranged to take the Swedes to western Hungary. I told him, too, to try stalling as long as possible. Then I hurried over to the general who was in charge of the only German garrison remaining in Budapest. With considerable trouble, I succeeded in gaining entry to the building and eventually got to speak with the general's adjutant. I explained the situation and asked for immediate action by the Germans to stop the ravages of the arrow crossmen. I told him we would hold the Germans responsible for what happened next. They held the power in the city, and if they did not support us, of course it would appear that the operation had been undertaken with their approval.

The adjutant regarded me coldly. Probably he was thinking that we had now gotten what we deserved. When I insisted on seeing the general, he went in and wakened his commander. But he quickly came back with the message that there was no point in my speaking with him. The general sent me the message that the German military could not intervene, since it was an internal, Hungarian matter. He advised me to contact the Hungarian military commandant of Budapest, General Hindy, instead.

I then went to the Hungarian headquarters and succeeded in gaining admittance. Hindy, a Hungarian officer of the old breed, with stiff bearing and a monocle in his eye, became agitated at my story but said he could not intervene without instructions from his government. Therefore, in my presence, he called the foreign ministry. It turned out to be a long conversation, during which the general's expression clouded over more and more. Gloomily, he hung up the receiver. "I am sorry, but unfortunately I cannot help you. The actions taken against the Swedish legation have been taken on orders from the highest level."

Leaving Hindy, I decided to go to the Swiss legation. I found Switzerland's chargé d'affaires, Secretary of Legation Feller, at home in his quarters, peacefully occupied with wrapping Christmas presents and decorating the tree. He became very upset over what had happened, and I am afraid my visit destroyed his Christmas celebration. Feller promised me all the support he could and at once put his staff to work to find out what had happened to the Swedes in the meantime. Eventually, we got the message that the minister and Wallenberg had succeeded in escaping at the last minute. Later that day, the minister turned up at the Swiss legation.

About the others, Asta Nilsson, Margareta Bauer, Ekmark, Berg and Carlsson, we knew nothing more than that they had been seized by the arrow crossmen. Rumor had it that both women had been taken away with a lot of Jews on the notorious road to Austria.

So the situation was grim and the chances of continued inquiry were curtailed by the heavy bombing attack on the city that had just begun. The final Russian offensive against Budapest was under way.

The Russian army coming from the south made, that day, a sudden and unexpected encircling movement, and in a few hours the connection with Vienna, open till then, was completely cut off. The Germans' evacuation was thereby rendered impossible. They were forced to stay and defend the city, which was completely contrary to the hopes of Budapest's people. The only bright spot for us was that this development was probably going to keep the arrow crossmen from shipping the Swedes out of the city. Fortunately, this is just what happened, and during the day Berg turned up. What had happened to him, briefly, was this:*

He and Carlsson had heard from the watchman at the Finnish legation that the arrow crossmen were breaking in and had immediately gone there. Berg went into the building but was unable to accomplish

* A detailed account of these events is to be found in Berg's book, *Vad hände i Budapest?* ("What Happened in Budapest?")

anything. When the arrow crossmen decreed that he would be sent to western Hungary, he pretended to agree to this. He only asked to be allowed to return to his lodgings and fetch his suitcases. This request was granted, and he got an armed arrow crossman as his escort.

Instead of heading for home, Berg with cool nerve drove directly to one of the German SS headquarters, and before his companion had time to realize what was happening, he jumped out of the car and informed the SS head of the Arrow Cross operation against the Swedish legation. He announced that, as chief of Department B, he had custody of the keys to the German legation in Budapest, whose personnel had already left the city, and so he requested German protection for his person. This was given at once. The arrow crossman was chased off by the SS head himself, and Berg was equipped with a document declaring that he and his property were under the protection of the Greater German Reich ("unter dem Schutze des Gross-deutschen Reiches").

Later on, we found this document extremely useful, making many copies of it and passing them out to the other members of our mission.

What had happened to Carlsson, Ekmark and the two ladies, Berg did not know. He and I now headed for a secret lodging that I had in the so-called Castle Hill district, the part of Buda where the Castle and most of the ministries were located. The apartment, which lay in a small two-story house on Uri Street, was known only to the members of our mission, and we decided to use it as a refuge in case of need.

We barricaded the door and sat down to wait. That

was one Christmas Eve I will never forget. Early the following morning, someone pounded on the door. We cocked our pistols and thought that the arrow crossmen had now found our hiding place. Imagine our joy when it turned out to be Carlsson instead! Not long after that, Ekmark turned up.

Carlsson related that he had been seized by the arrow crossmen outside the Finnish legation building and had been held under guard in our own legation along with Ekmark, whom they had also caught. Carlsson had succeeded in getting away by jumping out the window of the bathroom. Ekmark had been brought to the notorious Arrow Cross prison on Schwabenberg (Schwabian Hill) on the Buda side, but when, that same evening, the Russians launched an attack in the vicinity, he took advantage of the general confusion to escape.

Later, Wallenberg, too, came to my apartment. He had remained on the Pest side during the critical hours and in that way had escaped the Arrow Cross.

But Asta Nilsson and Margareta Bauer were missing and we were seriously worried over what might have happenéd to them. The next day, though, we got word that the Arrow Cross had locked them up in the city's ghetto. We heaved a sigh of relief that nothing worse had happened. After conferring with the Swiss, it was decided that Born, the Swiss Red Cross representative, would make an attempt to get the women out. Born, a daring man, took his car and drove to the ghetto, where in the name of the International Red Cross, in a tone of authority, he declared that he had orders to fetch two Swedes who had been brought there by mistake. This bold stroke succeeded, and the two were released.

They told us how the arrow crossmen had looted the legation buildings — the Finnish, totally, and our own, of clothing and food and the personal property of our staff. After that, the two women and a number of Jews had been marched under guard through the city to a barracks square, where all of them had been stood up against a wall. An arrow crossman announced that they would now be executed. The wall was pocked with bullet holes from previous executions.

Fortunately, the execution was not carried out, but instead the decision came that they would be brought to the ghetto to await deportation.

mais déporté

The Siege of Budapest.
Last Contact with Wallenberg

With the members of our mission together again, we held a council of war and decided first of all to try and retrieve the legation building from the arrow crossmen.

Wallenberg was the ingenious one. Through his good connections in the Ministry of the Interior, he succeeded in getting one of the higher officials there to put ten gendarmes at our disposal, who were given orders to take over the guarding of the legation. The gendarmes marched there and, while we discreetly remained in the background, announced to the disappointed arrow crossmen that the government had assigned them to relieve them. The arrow crossmen left and the gendarmes installed themselves as legation guards.

We realized that the legation could no longer continue its earlier activities, partly because the arrow crossmen were after us, and partly because heavy bombardment of the city had now begun both from the air and from Russian artillery that had gotten into position and surrounded the city. So it was necessary to go underground, in both senses.

In this connection, it did not seem advisable for all of us to stay in the same place. We judged the Swiss legation the safest refuge, since it was still respected by the arrow crossmen. It lay on Castle Hill and had a good air-raid shelter. The minister, Ekmark and the women settled there. I stayed in my apartment on Uri Street not far away, to be near the minister and to be able, when necessary, to get in touch with the German and Hungarian military leadership, who now kept to that part of the city. Wallenberg chose to stay on the Pest side, where his department had most of its offices and other locations. Berg and von Mezey were assigned the care of the legation building, with the help of the gendarme guards.

Those two were to face great danger during the final struggle and they deserve special praise for the bravery and quick-wittedness they displayed in risky situations. Berg, as mentioned earlier, had already been seasoned by service in Berlin. Von Mezey had, as a young man, taken part in World War I. For his bravery under fire he had, like many other Hungarians, had the word "Vitez," meaning Hero, attached to his name. It turned out that during this war, too, he would earn that epithet.

At first we were able to keep in touch with each other, though it was difficult. I visited the legation buildings now and then, and on a couple of occasions Berg came to see me. But toward the middle of January the bombardment became so unending that practically all connection between us became impossible.

Several of us escaped being hit by shells just by the skin of our teeth. The close calls were many. Berg related how he was about to go out in his car but had forgotten his overcoat. He went in to get it and when he came back the car had been hit by a shell and blown to bits.

Carlsson described how a burst of machine-gun fire

85

perforated the walls of the toilet he had visited only moments before. I myself was in my apartment when a surprise bombing raid took place. I never made it to the cellar but pressed up against the doorpost, which held, while the ceiling and its beams crashed down around me!

The last time I saw Wallenberg was the 10th of January, 1945. He paid me a brief visit and I remember how I pleaded insistently with him to suspend his operation and stay with us on the Buda side. The arrow crossmen were especially on the lookout for him, and he ran great risks by continuing his aid work. But Wallenberg would not listen to me.

While the bombs rained down around us, we sallied out to visit the headquarters of the German SS. There, among other matters, I was going to try and work out some sort of protection for members of the mission. Again and again we had to hit the brakes of the car, for the streets were blocked by dead bodies, horses, toppled trees and shattered buildings. But Wallenberg never hesitated at the danger. I asked him if he were not frightened. "Sure, it gets a little scary, sometimes," he said, "but for me there's no choice. I've taken on this assignment and I'd never be able to go back to Stockholm without knowing inside myself I'd done all a man could do to save as many Jews as possible."

During our visit to the SS general, Wallenberg was trying, among other things, to obtain guarantees that the Jews in the Swedish houses would not be liquidated at the last minute. As usual, Wallenberg stated his business skilfully and with intelligence. The SS general listened skeptically but found it hard to conceal that he was at the same time impressed by Wallenberg. I especially remember that part of the conversation in which the German suddenly put the following somewhat unexpected question to Wallenberg: "Sie kennen Gyula Dessewffy sehr gut? Er hat sich ja übrigens in Ihrem Haus versteckt!" ("You know Gyula Dessewffy very well, don't you. Matter of fact, he has hidden himself in your house!").

Dessewffy was a Hungarian aristocrat and journalist who had gone underground when the Germans marched in. He was, at this point, active in the Hungarian resistance movement and the Germans were searching for him eagerly. Dessewffy was known to the mission, but we had not been in touch with him for a long time. The day before the German occupation, on the 19th of March, 1944, he had taken his leave of me, saying he was going on a long journey. Only later did I learn this, but he and the resistance movement already knew what was about to happen.

Wallenberg became angered, of course, at the SS general's accusation and denied most emphatically that he was keeping Dessewffy hidden, and in this I chimed in.

Two years later, during my service in the legation in Cairo, I happened by chance to meet Dessewffy. After the war, he had become a member of the new Hungarian assembly. Now he was in Egypt with a delegation from Hungary's parliament and government to take part in an interparliamentary conference. The Communists had not, at that point, seized power and the majority in parliament was held by a liberal party, the Smallholders' Party, to which most of those in the delegation belonged.

We reminisced over old times in Hungary and I happened to mention the episode with the German SS general. "Of course I was at Wallenberg's," said Dessewffy. "But no one else was to know it. I thought that was best." For two weeks, he had stayed hidden in a little tower room on the other side of Wallenberg's garden, from which, unobserved, he could watch both Wallenberg and me, when I came to visit. The Germans had also known where Dessewffy was staying but had not dared to force their way into a Swedish diplomatic residence.

Since at the time when Dessewffy and his colleagues visited Cairo Hungary had not yet established diplomatic relations with Egypt — the Hungarian interests there were still looked after by our country — I got the chance to do my Hungarian friends one last service. On the day of his departure, Dessewffy came up to the legation with the diplomatic passports of his delegation. "Can you extend these?" he asked. All of them were still valid, but I understood. With the approval of my chief, Minister Bagge, I extended them for five years, for safety's sake. Some years later, I heard that, thanks to these passports, all the delegation members had been able to leave Hungary before the Communists, with Russian help, really took over.

Wallenberg's Last Acts,
His Unique Achievement

Wallenberg's words, the last time we saw each other, were typical of him and of the seriousness with which he took his assignment. "I'd never be able to go back to Stockholm without knowing inside myself I'd done all a man could do to save as many Jews as possible." And he did all that a man could, to the very last. He was tireless in his efforts to save Jews from deportation. Many are the stories of how he could pop up on the most unexpected occasions and succeed in preventing the removal of Jews with protective passports, or stop the arrow crossmen from forcing their way into the Swedish houses. He swamped the Arrow Cross authorities with written petitions for relief for his charges. It was often he who was the prime mover in the neutral legations' protests, through joint memoranda, to the Arrow Cross regime, against the inhuman treatment of the Jews.

Even if the mass deportations to Auschwitz by rail had stopped, the Germans made sporadic attempts to ship groups of Jews off by train.

Wallenberg always had people on watch who could warn him in time to get to the station before the train's departure. On one occasion, he arrived with several long lists of the holders of protective passports and demanded in an authoritative tone to check whether any such persons had by mistake been taken aboard. The Germans were taken by surprise and, right under their noses, Wallenberg pulled out a large number of Jews. Many of them had no passport at all, only various papers in the Hungarian language — drivers licenses, vaccination records or tax receipts — that the Germans did not understand. The bluff succeeded.

Another time, when I was there, the Germans tried to stop us with guns. But we stood our ground, showed our Swedish diplomatic passports, and were able to leave with our charges.

One day when Wallenberg was elsewhere, I rushed out to a station from which a trainload of Jews was about to depart. There was no time to debate with the Germans. I explained that a terrible mistake had been made, since apparently they were about to deport Jews who had Swedish protective passports. Should they not be released immediately, I would make sure that Veesenmayer was informed. The reaction to this proved to be the same as on the tenth of October, when we were sending home the group of Swedish women and children. The German train commander did not dare to risk being reported to the dreaded Veesenmayer. I went into the cars to call the roll, but found only two Jews with protective passports. However, with the help of the Hungarian police officer there, Batizfalvy (who secretly cooperated with Raoul Wallenberg and me), I succeeded, despite the SS commandant's orders, in freeing 150 Jews from the station even though 148 had no protective passports.

Wallenberg sometimes arranged for special expeditions in which Jews who looked Aryan, dressed in Arrow Cross uniforms, raided camps and prisons and on several occasions succeeded in freeing a large

90

number of Jews on the pretext that they were being taken away to deportation.

How many persons did Wallenberg save? To that question, a clear-cut answer can hardly be given.

I witnessed his stopping the deportation of a total of several thousand Jews at train stations, from the Swedish houses, and during the death march to the Austrian border.

It was through these acts that the rumor was spread of his almost superhuman ability, in seemingly hopeless situations, to snatch victims from the Nazi executioners. He became hated but feared by the arrow crossmen. He became the Budapest Jews' hope of rescue from the final liquidation.

Yet it was not through the kind of personal intervention just described that he made his greatest contribution. It was as a negotiator that he achieved his greatest results. He was the driving force behind the agreements entered into with the Arrow Cross regime concerning their respecting not only the 5,000 Swedish protective passports but also corresponding documents of the other neutral legations.

Wallenberg was always conscious of the fact that saving as *many* persons as possible was what mattered. "You know yourself," he remarked on one occasion, "how we're besieged every day by people who plead for a job at the legation, for asylum or for a protective passport for themselves and their relations. When they can't come themselves, they send their Aryan friends to ask help for them. All of them want to meet me personally. I've got to be firm. Time doesn't allow me to devote myself to single cases when it's a question of life or death for Budapest's entire Jewish population."

Wallenberg held to this line rigorously.

To accomplish his ends, he applied every means. He bribed Arrow Cross officials. Sometimes he threatened execution. Other times he promised pardon after the arrival of the Russians. He used Foreign Minister Kemény's wife (who was of Jewish descent and greatly admired him) to influence her husband to approve the protective passports and so on.

As I mentioned earlier, after the war had ended, it was established that 50,000 Jews who lived in the foreign houses, the international ghetto, had survived. They were generally equipped with protective passports or similar documents issued by the neutral legations and the International Red Cross. Of these, Wallenberg had protected nearly half, around 20 to 25,000.

But Wallenberg's contribution extended even further. Besides his efforts for the international ghetto, toward the end he also worked to protect the inhabitants of Budapest's general or so-called sealed ghetto, where around 70,000 had been forced together. He could sometimes arrange for food deliveries to the starving, and he managed on several occasions to forestall the arrow crossmen's rampages in the ghetto.

But the arrow crossmen had, in their fanatical hatred of the Jews, decided to commit mass murder in the ghetto at the last minute. When Wallenberg got wind of this, he demanded that the German commander, General Schmidthuber, prevent the killing. Otherwise, Wallenberg would make sure that

92

Schmidthuber would swing on the gallows when the Russians came.

Schmidthuber was shaken by Wallenberg's words and stopped the planned operation against the ghetto.

Thus Wallenberg contributed to saving still another 70,000 lives.

Jenö Lévai, in his book, *Raoul Wallenberg – Hero of Budapest*, praises Wallenberg's efforts for the Jews in the sealed ghetto. He adds: "It is of the utmost importance that the Nazis and the arrow crossmen were not able to ravage unhindered — they were compelled to see that every step they took was being watched and followed by the young Swedish diplomat. From Wallenberg they could keep no secrets. The arrow crossmen could not trick him. They could not operate freely, they were held responsible for the lives of the persecuted and the condemned. Wallenberg was the 'world's observing eye,' the one who continually called the criminals to account.

"That is the great importance of Wallenberg's struggle in Budapest."

To Rescue a Nobel Prizewinner

During the last days of 1944, I shared my place on Uri Street with a Hungarian who became one of my best friends, namely, the Nobel prizewinner, Professor Albert Szent-Györgyi. He was one of the prominent figures in the Hungarian resistance movement. With his good international connections, he was regarded by many as made-to-order for the job of Hungarian chief of state after the war. A more detailed account of his dramatic escape from the Nazis is in order, especially since it so happened that the mission came to be deeply involved in his rescue.

In 1943 Szent-Györgyi had, by his own account, secretly contacted the British authorities during a visit to Istanbul. He confided in them that all the Hungarian political parties except the Nazis were willing to accept him as the leader of Hungary, in connection with the Germans' anticipated collapse on the eastern front. If the Allies meant to allow Hungary to survive and play a constructive role in the rebuilding of Europe, he was at their service. On the Hungarian side, they were prepared to try hastening the German defeat through acts of sabotage.

The British obviously attached some weight to the contact with Szent-Györgyi, a respected, internationally known scientist who was, in foreign policy terms, neutral. True, the answer was the same as given to earlier, similar probes. As long as the Hungarians continued to take part in the war on the Axis side, they could not expect any sympathy or understanding, no matter what proposals they made. Yet, a certain change was noticeable. Great Britain had no wish to see Hungary go under or to punish the Hungarian people for those mistakes their government had made. The attitude of the Allies depended on what Hungary was able to do, on her own, to break the alliance with the Germans.

Unfortunately, though, the German Gestapo got wind of Szent-Györgyi's activities. Hitler became enraged and was further reinforced in his conviction that Hungary intended to "jump ship."

After returning from Istanbul, Szent-Györgyi returned to his university in Szeged in eastern Hungary. When the Germans occupied, he was forced to flee from there and stay in hiding, at first in Budapest. His friends feared that the Gestapo would soon find his hiding place and got in touch with the legation to see if we had any chance to rescue him. As soon as we reported the matter to our Foreign Office, Szent-Györgyi quickly received Swedish citizenship. However, this was not much help, since the Germans refused to honor any foreign citizenship granted after they had occupied Hungary on the 19th of March, 1944. So we decided to hide Szent-Györgyi for the time being at the mission's evacuation place, Enying, by Lake Balaton. In disguise and under an assumed name, he functioned there officially as the mission's filing clerk, which could be justified by our already having transferred the greater part of our archives there. Szent-Györgyi played the role to perfection. He had let his beard grow, put on large horn-rimmed glasses and, in our eyes, made a convincing impression.

The summer went by, and the work of "filing" was not so pressing that he could not manage to complete a research paper that was sent, with the aid of the legation, to Stockholm for publication in a scientific journal.

In September, however, we began to be worried about Szent-Györgyi's safety. The Germans had gotten on the trail of the Hungarian resistance movement and, in a raid, captured and executed several of its leaders.

The resistance movement had, with Horthy's approval, been in touch with the Allies about a plan to land British paratroopers in Hungary at the same time that the Hungarians turned their guns on the Germans. In this matter, Szent-Györgyi had been Horthy's intermediary. As things turned out, the plan never jelled. However, Horthy had decided to try and get a cease-fire with the Soviets at the earliest opportunity.

One day, Szent-Györgyi confided in us that, without our knowledge, he had been brought to Horthy for discussions. In the course of this talk it came out that they intended to send Szent-Györgyi, with a member of the government or an officer of high rank, by plane to Moscow for negotiations toward a cease-fire. Everything was ready for the departure when Horthy all of a sudden changed his mind, and Szent-Györgyi had to return to Enying with his mission unaccomplished. The reason was supposed to have been that the Germans had gotten suspicious and this had obliged Horthy to give up the plan.

The Elizabeth and Chain bridges before they were blown up in January, 1945.

Raoul Wallenberg.

The author by the Danube in the summer of 1943.

The first Jews
seeking help, outside
the Swedish Legation
in March, 1944.

The Finnish Legation after bombing raids.

Jews drafted to clear rubble after the bombings of Budapest.

Berg ready for an expedition.

Outside the Swedish Legation. On the left, von Mezey on watch.

Arrow crossmen outside the Swedish Legation in January, 1945.

Minister Danielsson.

Protective passport issued by the Swedish Legation.

The Swedish mission on their return to Stockholm. Left to right, Ivan Danielsson, Margareta Bauer, Denes von Mezey, Elena Anger and the author.

Igazolvány

A Svéd Kir. Követség igazolja, hogy

DR MAGASDI MIKLÓS

tisztviselője

Budapest, 1944. november 25.

Svéd Kir. Követségi titkár.

Legitimation

Die Kgl. Schwedische Gesandtschaft
bestätigt hiemit, dass

Nikolaus MAGASDI

Beamter der Gesandtschaft ist.

Budapest, den 25. November 1944.

Kgl. Schwedischer Gesandtschaftssekretär

Aláírás — Unterschrift

Identification papers
issued by Wallenberg to
members of his Jewish
staff.

KÖNIGLICH
SCHWEDISCHE GESANDTSCHAFT

BESCHEINIGUNG.
- - - - - - - - - - - - - -

Die Kgl. Schwedische Gesandtschaft bescheinigt hiermit, dass

Frau Nikolaus M A G A S D I
geb. Eva Bolt

Ehefrau des bei der Kgl. Schwedischen
Gesandtschaft ständig arbeitenden Herrn
Dr.Nikolaus Magasdi ist.

Budapest, den 15. August 1944.

Kgl. Schwedischer Gesandtschaftssekretär.

Name

I G A Z O L V Á N Y .
- - - - - - - - - - - - - -

A Svéd Kir.Követség iga-

zolja, hogy

dr. M A G A S D I Miklósné urnő

felesége a Svéd Kir.Követségen állandóan

dolgozó dr. Magasdi Miklós urnak.

Budapest, 1944 augusztus 15.

Wallenberg s.k.
Svéd Kir. Követségi Titkár.

ШВЕДСКОЕ КОРОЛЕВСКОЕ ПОСОЛЬСТВО
ЗАЩИТНИК ИНТЕРЕСОВ
СССР
В ВЕНГРИИ

Настоящим официально удостоверяется, что

Биргит БРУЛИН

является сотрудником Шведского Королевского Посольства в Будапеште

и как он сам, так и его семья, а также квартира: Budapest Minerva u. 1 a

состоят под защитой Шведского Королевского Посольства.

Будапешт, 1-ое ноября 1944 г.

Шведский Кор. Посол.

Identification document in Russian, issued to
Birgit Brulin by the Swedish Legation.

KÖNIGLICH
SCHWEDISCHE GESANDTSCHAFT
BUDAPEST

A Külföldieket Ellenőrző Orsz. Közp. Hatóságnak,

B u d a p e s t.

Van szerencsénk közölni, hogy a budapesti Svéd Kir. Követség

részére védőútlevelet állított ki, melynek értelmében nevezett svéd
alattvalónak tekintendő.

Tisztelettel kéri a Követség, sziveskedjenek nevezettnek a meg-
különböztető jelzés viselése alól való mentességet megadni. Igazolja a
Követség, hogy a vonatkozó rendeletben emlitett viszonosság Svédország-
gal fennáll.

Budapest, 1944.

Kiváló tisztelettel

R.: ....

Sp.: ....

Svéd kir. követ helyett
Svéd kir. követségi titkár.

Form used by the Royal Swedish Legation for informing the Hungarian authorities that the person mentioned is entitled to be treated as
a Swedish national

There was a great risk that Szent-Györgyi's hideout would be discovered, and I was given the assignment of fetching him and taking him to my apartment. Since I did not trust the doorman of my building, who had given signs of suspecting something, Szent-Györgyi lived with me only a few days and then moved to the legation. To keep the Hungarian servants from suspecting anything, he received the name "Svensson" and was said to be a bombed-out Swedish businessman from southern Hungary, who had gotten temporary housing with us. Szent-Györgyi lived at the legation for two months and during that time we felt relatively sure of his safety. We taught him some of the essential Swedish words, including "skål," which we used assiduously whenever any of the Hungarian servants was around.

We speculated about what would happen after the Russians came. With Szent-Györgyi's help, after reorganizing the legation, we would be able to continue our activities, in general, and in particular to relieve the victims of the war. Surely the Russians would show understanding. We looked forward to the crushing of the Nazis and the takeover by the Russians. Those reports we received from the Hungarian foreign ministry about atrocities the Russian soldiers had committed against the civilian population, on invading Hungary, we took with a grain of salt. We were prepared to dismiss these reports as the usual Nazi horror stories. But events would prove that, for once, the foreign ministry was right. Things turned out differently than what we expected.

Rumors began to go around town that Professor Szent-Györgyi had managed to get over to the Russian side and that he had set up a new Hungarian government, with its seat in the city of Debrecen. We hastened to support the rumors. But one day Brunhoff, who was the German Counselor of Legation, called me up. I knew him from his earlier service in Stockholm. Couldn't we get together for lunch? I understood that he had something on his mind.

After we had sat and chatted for a while about everyday things, suddenly he said: "You know Professor Szent-Györgyi, don't you?" Summoning all my resources of self-control, I answered that I didn't know him very well, but of course I knew his name, since he was a winner of the Swedish Nobel Prize. The German looked me right in the eye and continued: "Rumors are circulating that he's over with the Russians, but that's not so. He's staying in Budapest, and I know where."

That was a warning if ever there was one. I began to understand why the German sentries on Gellért Hill above the legation had lately been giving us such special attention. With their field glasses, they usually kept the legation garden under observation. Probably Szent-Györgyi, who was an avid outdoorsman, had tired of being shut up inside and, on some occasion, despite our strict admonition to stay inside, had taken a walk in the garden and there been seen by the Germans. Another possibility was that one of the servants had discovered "Svensson's" real identity and reported it to the Gestapo.

Szent-Györgyi could now stay with us no longer. Even if the legation enjoyed extraterritorial rights in principle, it was still uncertain what the Gestapo might do when it came to capturing such a rare bird as Szent-Györgyi. When, after the German occupation, former prime minister Kállay had made his escape to the Turkish legation, the Turks had been forced to hand him over by the threat that otherwise he would be taken by force. Nothing prevented the Germans from treating us the same way. Another hiding place for him would have to be found. The same day, we managed to find one in Pest, where I took him that night in my car. When the siege of the city had begun and it looked as though Buda would be the first to fall to the Russians, I decided to move Szent-Györgyi to my place on Uri Street on Castle Hill, where he would come in contact with the Russians sooner.

Szent-Györgyi's son-in-law, George Libik, a resistance fighter whom I came to know, handled the transfer. He served secretly as our chauffeur and was a great help to me and the mission in many precarious situations. (Libik succeeded in leaving Hungary during the 1956 revolution and is now active as a businessman in Stockholm.)

In the beginning of January, 1945, though, it became plain that Buda, and especially the area around the Castle, was the part of the city that was going to hold out the longest against the Russians. Therefore my guest was moved one last time. Just before the bridges over the Danube were blown up, I asked Libik to take him over to the Pest side once again.

Later we learned that Szent-Györgyi, after the Russian conquest of Pest, had quickly made contact with Marshal Malinovsky's headquarters. He then spent some time in Moscow. But soon after his return to Hungary, he ended up in opposition to the Hungarian Communist Party and the Russian occupying forces as well, when he decried their arrests and brutalities. At a meeting with Stalin in 1946 he is said to have demanded that the Hungarian military who had committed war crimes be tried before Hungarian courts and not be deported by the thousands to the Gulag.

Libik has related that he later met Szent-Györgyi, who expressed his disgust with the Soviet system and said, word-for-word: "He (Stalin) is a bloodthirsty murderer, a thousand times worse than Hitler."

Szent-Györgyi explained that he intended to leave Hungary immediately, not to return until the Russians had left. Through the then Interior Minister Rajk (later executed), Libik was able to arrange an extension of Szent-Györgyi's passport. Disillusioned, Szent-Györgyi left his country, which had placed such great hopes in him.

Szent-Györgyi now lives in the United States, where he devotes his time entirely to science.

The Swedish Government Expels the Arrow Cross Representative; Consequences for the Legation

At least the intensifying bombardment had this to be said for it — we could feel safer from the arrow crossmen. They generally displayed no great bravery in moments of danger and dared not go out in the rain of projectiles. Besides, they were so occupied with their continuing operation against the Jews that they found no time to search for a handful of Swedes. However, there was still considerable risk of attack when one went out into the town, especially in Pest, where the arrow crossmen were the most active just then. Even the Swiss risked being attacked by the armed bands.

One day the Swiss Secretary of Legation, Feller, returned badly beaten from a visit to Pest. He told me that the arrow crossmen stopped his car and dragged him to their headquarters on Andrássy Boulevard. There he was beaten so brutally that he lost consciousness. When he came to, he heard the arrow crossmen say that he was going to be taken to the "cold room," a very sophisticated torture chamber from which few came back alive, and that the Swedish minister would experience the same fate as soon as they got their hands on him.

Then Feller had an inspiration that probably saved him. "Of course you can take my life," he said, "but then I can guarantee that your 'minister' in Bern will be swinging on the gallows tomorrow." The arrow crossmen released Feller at once.

That is, Switzerland, in contrast to Sweden, had allowed a Szálasi representative, a consul, to remain in Bern for the time being. It was this card that Feller, with great presence of mind, had played.

After that, Feller succeeded in getting on a good footing with the arrow crossmen, to all our advantage. By continuing to point to the presence of an Arrow Cross representative in Bern, he could maintain the appearance of good relations between the Arrow Cross regime and the Swiss government. As for us, we were reminded of the action of the Swedish Foreign Office in expelling the Arrow Cross representative, Vöczköndy, on short notice. It was Vöczköndy who directed the attack on the legation on Christmas Eve, 1944. I cannot help but agree with the writer Rudolph Philipp when, in the Swedish magazine "Vi" for January 14, 1955, he said:

"In Stockholm, the change of government in Budapest led to the appointment as Szálasi's chargé d'affaires of the man who had till then been the assistant military attaché. Just at that time there were plenty of bandits accredited as diplomats in Stockholm, which was swarming with Nazi diplomats of various nationalities. This Nazi, too, could just as well have been treated with courtesy a few weeks more, if we were really serious about the attempt to save the surviving Hungarian Jews from total destruction. Both the USA, whose president had taken the initiative for Raoul Wallenberg's rescue mission, and the Soviet Union, whose interests in Hungary were being minded by Sweden, would surely have shown the greatest understanding for such tolerance. Yet only toward the Hungarian fascists did his excellency Mr. Gunther take action. Szálasi's representative was thrown out of Sweden!

"To expel another country's chargé d'affaires is a pretty clear message that you don't want any 'diplomatic relations' with that country. Even so, our Foreign Office made no move to call home Raoul Wallenberg or our mission in general, despite having by this brusque move pulled the juridical rug out from under both Raoul's rescue assignment as a neutral diplomat and the mission's activities as the sheltering power for Allied and Russian citizens. The Foreign Office's action, and its passivity thereafter, completely abandoned our Swedish diplomats as private citizens to the tender mercies of the Arrow Cross regime!"

There is also not a shred of doubt that it was the Foreign Office's action in expelling Vöczköndy and the Swedish government's stiff-necked unwillingness to recognize the Szálasi regime that set off the operation against our legation. If the Russians had not arrived at just that time, the consequences for the Jews in the Swedish houses would have been terrible. In all probability, the arrow crossmen, having discovered that no recognition by the Swedish government was to be had, would have carried out their threats and blown the Swedish houses with their tenants to kingdom come, or liquidated them in some other way. All the Swedish efforts would have been in vain.

In telegram after telegram during the fall of 1944, Danielsson pointed out the importance of extending some kind of recognition to the Szálasi government in order to make continued rescue work possible. Besides Switzerland — we pointed out — Turkey and Spain, too, had accepted Szálasi's representatives in their countries, whereby their missions in Budapest could go on working undisturbed. But the answer from Sweden was a categorical No.

It is hard to find an explanation for this stiff-legged policy, through which not only the legation's existence but also, above all, the lives of our Jewish charges were placed in danger. It can hardly have been out of consideration for the Allies that we refused to recognize Szálasi. They would certainly have accepted an explanation by Sweden that recognition of the Arrow Cross was necessary in order to save the Jews.

The Russians Conquer
Pest, Buda Totters

The Russians had now closed the ring around Budapest. When their attack on Buda was temporarily stopped by the Germans' stubborn defense, they decided to deliver the decisive blow from another direction. One day in the middle of January, 1945, they made a sudden thrust with large forces through Pest. Advancing swiftly, in part underground through the cellars of the lodging houses that in Pest generally connected with one another, the Russians quickly seized that part of the city. The Germans were taken by surprise and only managed to get a few of their troops across to the Buda side, blowing up the bridges behind them.

At this point, only the Szent-Gellért heights, Castle Hill and Rose Hill still remained in German hands. From now on, we were able from our place on Castle Hill to see with unaided eye the Russian soldiers on the opposite side of the river. The bombardment increased every day, and Buda was now subjected to direct machine-gun fire from across the river.

One day I had to go through a baptism of fire. I was sitting in the Swiss legation building chatting with the secretary of the legation and two Hungarians who had been through the fighting on the eastern front and were what you call hardened veterans. It had been a relatively peaceful day, but suddenly we heard how the Russian artillery was approaching. Before we

113

knew it, the shelling had reached our block. I thought the shells crashed down first on one side of the building and then on the other, and expected the room we sat in to get a direct hit at any moment. The atmosphere was charged and I felt very uncomfortable.

Suddenly one of the Hungarians rose and said: "I think I'll cross the room and fetch my overcoat, because if the room tears apart, I'll be without it." Seconds later, the foundations of the building were rocked by a powerful explosion. We hurled ourselves down the stairs to the yard and into a nearby cellar, which under the prevailing conditions had been fitted out for a pig sty. In the dark, we fell over the frightened pigs, which sprang in every direction. "Open your mouth!" somebody said, "saves your eardrums." There we stood through half an hour's terrible drumfire accompanied by the grunting of the pigs. When we came out into daylight at last, the room where we had sat before was gone.

The situation of Buda's inhabitants got worse by the day. The supply of electricity, gas and water gradually ceased. Because of the bombings and the shooting it was nearly impossible to remain outdoors. In the old historic vaulted cellars built in the time of the Turks, and in other buildings in the Castle Hill district, there were some ten thousand persons who had taken refuge there in December when the struggle for Budapest itself began. The fact is, the city was otherwise extraordinarily unprovided with air raid shelters. Starving, they had lived there for a month now, men, women and children right in the middle of military staffs and units. I passed one of these cellars when I occasionally visited the Swiss Red Cross representative, who had established an underground hospital nearby. The distress of these people was very great. The stench that met one there was indescribable.

The conditions in the underground hospital were pitiful. Wounded soldiers took up every inch of space. There was the greatest scarcity of medicine, the doctors operating and amputating by candlelight, most often without any anaesthetics.

One day, two badly wounded American pilots were brought in. They had been shot down over Budapest. One of them, just before he lost consciousness, uttered the word "penicillin." That antibiotic was then practically unknown in Hungary. Not even the hospital had access to it. By telegraphing Stockholm and coordinating with the Swiss, we managed to get some penicillin brought through Switzerland by courier just a day or two before Budapest was cut off from the outside world. With this shipment, the doctors succeeded in saving the lives not only of the two Americans but of other severely wounded persons as well.

In the building where I lived, we kept ourselves going thanks to a few canned goods we had managed to hide away, and our daily diet usually consisted of a thin soup. Luckily, there was a wood stove in the house. After the kitchen was bombed, we succeeded in pulling the stove out of the debris and standing it up in the yard, where the owner of the house, a Hungarian baroness with great contempt for death, took over the cooking. It was the men's assignment to fetch water, which was to be found in a reservoir in a square nearby that lay wide open to Russian gunfire. When we crouched down to chop a hole in the ice and fill our buckets with dirty yellow water that had really been intended for putting out fires and not for household use, the bullets spattered the ice all around us. I heaved a sigh of relief every time I succeeded in returning on the run with the water pails.

One day we got our menu augmented in an unexpected way. During an air raid, a horse that belonged to a nearby German unit happened to get shot right before our door. We were not slow to join the swarm of people who hurried from all directions, brandishing knives and other instruments, to get themselves a piece of horse meat. It was a macabre sight. Old and young, women in furs and poor laborers, all crowded eagerly around the cadaver of the horse, attempting to chop off the largest piece they could. In a short while, nothing was left of it but bones. We lived for several days on Hungarian horse goulash, skilfully prepared by the baroness.

There were other occasions just as unpleasant as fetching water. Even though none of us had then heard of Gabriel Chevallier's book, *House of Unease*, we had given a similar name to the corresponding facilities on the upper floor of our house. Whenever anyone went up there, it always seemed as if the Russian gunfire intensified. An accident almost happened, one time, when the baroness' sister, a somewhat corpulent lady, went up there to the toilet. A shell struck the upper floor, the beams and shingles tumbling down into the yard with a great crash. I happened to be standing at the entrance to the cellar and saved myself by throwing myself heedlessly down the stairs. Later, as soon as we could, we made our way upstairs to rescue the sister. We were prepared

116

for the worst but, happily, nothing serious had happened. The shock of the shell's impact had thrown her out the door of the toilet and she landed on a divan in the next room. We found her dazed but unharmed.

Up to this time I had continued to live above ground, like the other occupants of the house, and had only gone down to the cellar when the air raids turned toward our part of the city or the artillery bombardment got too heavy. The air raid warning was not being given any more, since the sirens, to the extent that they were still functioning, would now have had to sound without pause. On our street, warning was so arranged that a lookout rang a bell whenever he thought the enemy planes were heading for our own neighborhood. This system was not especially effective, but eventually one learned to distinguish those sounds that meant danger.

A German soldier whom I sometimes chatted with once said, reassuringly, when a bomb had fallen beside us: "Whenever you hear that whistling sound before the bomb hits, there's usually no danger, because the bomb isn't falling right on you. It's only when you don't hear anything beforehand that it's falling on your own head, and then, *so wie so*, there's not much you can do about it."

The Russian daily program was repeated punctually. In the morning, the Russian fighter planes came in low over Buda, where there was no longer any air defense to speak of, and swept the streets with their machine guns. After that, the Russian rocket launchers, the "Stalin organs," went to work. The terrible projectiles smashed down in rows with an earsplitting crash. Streets and squares were swept clean of all life by the shock wave, and the doors and windows of houses were pushed in. In the afternoon artillery fire began, and towards evening the bombing attack, which is what we most feared. Even though the Russians did not usually drop the heavier sort of bombs, we were uncertain that our "air raid shelter," a rather deep but otherwise quite ordinary firewood and potato cellar, could withstand a direct hit. There was always the possibility of going down in the public cellars I described earlier, but we were understandably loath to do that.

One house after another on the Buda side was pounded to bits by the Russian projectiles. (According to statistics published after the war, of the 789 buildings in Buda, only 4 remained relatively undamaged.)

The Swiss' building as well as our own were hit time after time. Winter conditions made the situation worse. It snowed heavily in January and what was left of the buildings was further destroyed by the wet. Now we were forced to move down in the cellar for good, where, despite the cold and damp, we managed to make it tolerably comfortable. Separation into ladies' quarters and men's quarters was out of the question; we lived like cave men with one problem overshadowing all others — survival. Our conversation mainly concerned how long it would be till the Russians came and whether the food supply would last.

It is interesting to observe how different people react differently in moments of danger. The baroness' servant girl mostly huddled, scared to death, in a corner of the cellar, while her mistress stood ramrod-straight preparing our food. Some concealed their fear by activity of some kind, a forced chatter or hysterical laughter, and others by an increasing taciturnity.

It began to be plain that the resistance to the Russians could not go on much longer. However, there was no sign that the Germans intended to draw back from Buda voluntarily. They prepared themselves for defense among the ruins and probably intended to sell their lives as dearly as possible, after the pattern of Stalingrad. Since we saw no point in such a struggle, which would only lead to continued bloodshed, on a couple of occasions we and the Swiss contacted the German commander and the Hungarian commander, General Hindy, intending to persuade them to surrender. We offered to try and arrange contact with the Russians. They responded that they had no intention whatsoever of giving up the city. They intended to fight to the last.

Later on, we learned that the German commander had sent a message by telegraph to Hitler, requesting to be allowed to surrender. But Hitler had vetoed this: "Die Stadt muss bis zum letzten Mann gehalten werden" ("The city must be held to the last man") was his typical reply.

When we realized that there was no hope of accomplishing anything in that way, we, like the Swiss, began to think about trying to evacuate to the third hill, Rozadomb (Rose Hill), which lay somewhat nearer the Russian lines. From there, we would more quickly fall into Russian hands and avoid remaining in the Castle Hill district during the final bitter struggle. The Swiss legation building had by that time been bombed some fifty times, and to stay above ground was getting harder and harder. Besides, there was a risk that the Russians would start dropping bombs of heavier caliber, against which the cellars would provide no protection. The food supply was also becoming increasingly difficult. Ekmark and I were given the assignment of reconnoitering for a possible move, and especially checking whether the evacuation refuges that we and the Swiss had established on Rose Hill were still habitable. We set out early one morning at the end of January, 1945, on what under normal conditions would have been half an hour's stroll. It now took us half a day, a difficult journey during which I often doubted we would get through with our lives. We climbed over overturned cars and wagons and around bomb craters. Again and again we had to throw ourselves down to escape the machine gun fire of the Russian fighter planes that came flashing over us at low altitude.

Meeting the Russians

Just as we arrived at the legation's building on Rose Hill, we were subjected to heavy fire from some Russian "Stalin organs" on the other side of the river. By hastily crouching down we came through it with whole skins and arrived, shaken, at the legation's evacuation place on Sàrólta Street. We found our building partly damaged, but the bottom floor as well as the air raid shelter were still inhabitable. We realized that the place would no longer accommodate a larger number of persons, and the same applied to the Swiss building next door, which had sustained a similar degree of damage in the air raids. A report was sent to Danielsson in which we dissuaded both him and the Swiss from trying, under the circumstances, to evacuate to Rose Hill. Even the trip there was, in our judgment, too risky. However, we ourselves decided to stay there and observe what was going to happen.

The building lay near the front itself, and we ought rather soon to be on the Russian side. Thereby, perhaps we would get the chance to let the Russians know where the foreign missions in Buda were located.

Several days later, Carlsson, too, joined us.

Strangely enough, the telephone connections on Rose Hill still functioned here and there, though sporadically. One of the neighbors told us how he had gotten a call from an acquaintance not so far away.

Suddenly, the other had interrupted the conversation with: "Now I see through the window how the Russians are coming into the garden," whereupon the line went dead. The Russians had quickly cut the telephone wire that the Germans for some reason had overlooked.

A period of intensive artillery and aerial bombardment now tried our nerves. The Swiss legation's evacuation building, the so-called Franz Joseph Palace, now received such extensive damage that the Swiss most certainly could not have used it for a refuge. One day, the house next door to us was completely demolished. Ekmark, as an old artilleryman, estimated the caliber of the shells as at least 150-millimeter. There was no doubt that our house, too, would have been leveled if it had been hit. Even our shelter's ability to withstand an impact was debatable under such conditions.

In the cellar, two houses away, lay the Turkish military attaché with a broken back. He had happened to be on the Margareta Bridge that day last November, a month or so before the Russian attack, when the bridge had been blown up by mistake. He had been thrown into the Danube in his car. He had been rescued, but now he found himself in a seemingly hopeless condition. We visited him between the bombings but could not be of much help.

During the following week the Russians started getting closer. On the 29th of January, we could hear the machine guns distinctly and realized that the street fighting had reached our block. During all this time we had neither radio nor telephone. Later, I read a communique from Moscow that spoke of an unceasing, bitter struggle from house to house, from yard to yard, from block to block, comparable only with the battle for Stalingrad.

The German infantry withdrew, fighting, across Rose Hill, and one day a platoon of weary, frozen and dejected German soldiers arrived and began digging their gun emplacements in our garden. It was not especially appealing to be brought right into the line of fire, and so I went out to explain to the commander that he was on extraterritorial ground and so should try to set up his defense some other place. He looked at me pityingly and explained that "Krieg ist Krieg" ("War is war") and that they respectfully didn't give a damn if they were in the Swedish legation's garden. This spot was, from a defensive standpoint, the best they could get for the moment. Besides, he said, we should not despair. Rose Hill would be successfully defended against the Russian attack, and it was only a question of time until they would throw the Russians out of Hungary. Strong German reinforcements were marching toward Budapest, and there was no doubt that the Germans would win the war in the end.

Of course I was not inspired by the words of the German commander, but that very same evening the Germans withdrew from our garden and then we understood that the Russians could not be far away. In the evening I went out and raised the Swedish flag, which we had not dared to fly till now for fear of the arrow crossmen. I also placed a sign on the door in the Russian language with the text *Swedish Legation*. At the same time, I removed the nameplate of the former tenant which said "Hauptmann Klinger." That is, a German officer had happened to live in the house before us, and since his nameplate gave excellent protection from the arrow crossmen we had intentionally left it in place.

The next morning, which was the 30th of January, 1945, I was awakened by the janitor who, with loud cries, proclaimed that something was afoot. "Herr Attaché, Herr Attaché, einige Soldaten sind da" (". . . there are some soldiers here"). I answered drowsily that he should let me sleep in peace because it was very likely German soldiers who had come back. "Oh no, it's not Germans," he explained. "They're talking some other language."

So the Russians had come! I rushed upstairs from the shelter, where we spent our nights, excited at this first meeting.

In the kitchen stood two smart-looking Russian soldiers wearing white parkas and armed with submachine guns. They looked around curiously. Ekmark and I were not at all smart-looking! We had let our beards grow and were rather ungroomed after our month-long cellar sojourn. We had lived more or less in the belief that the less elegant we were, the better our reception by the Russians would be.

The soldiers looked at us suspiciously. They probably thought we were wanted men who were trying to masquerade in some way. They began to pick up small objects of value that they found in the kitchen, right under the nose of the outraged janitor, a true Hungarian democrat who had never expected such behavior from the Russian "liberators." We greeted the Russians heartily and showed them our identification cards, which we had had prepared in the Russian language. They studied these very closely and after conferring a moment they left.

Ekmark and I were pleasantly surprised by this apparently happy outcome of our meeting with the Russians. We felt relief that the war, for our part, seemed to be over, and poured the last drops out of a cognac bottle to raise a *skål* to our "liberators." We did not have time to consummate this toast, however, before there was a hammering on the door and a Russian noncom with Mongolian features stalked in. He was followed by a score of soldiers who looked around the house greedily.

I went up to them with a somewhat strained smile and again showed my identification card. The Russian examined it and looked disappointed. Apparently he had intended to billet himself and his men in the house. That all this belonged to the Swedish legation was a disappointment. He left, muttering angrily, and we had an unpleasant impression he was going to come back. Sure enough, after a moment he was back again and declared that we should come with him, that "the general" wanted to speak with us.

We suspected this about "the general" was a ruse. Ekmark went along, but I stayed to watch the house. After a moment, Ekmark returned, followed by the now highly indignant Russian noncom. "The Russians want the house," said Ekmark, "and they want a watch, too. But since I haven't one on me, you'll probably have to give them yours instead."

Meanwhile, the Russian accosted me, with that characteristic phrase we would later hear so often: "Daváy! Daváy!" ("Give it to me!"). Since I wasn't especially eager to present him with my wristwatch, I at first pretended not to understand what he meant. He repeated his demand, and I held out my fountain pen, hoping he would be satisfied with that. But my offer was taken as a direct affront and the Russian slapped his pistol holster threateningly, while making it clear by sign and gesture that he wanted something round that ticked. The pantomime also conveyed that if he didn't get it he would shoot, and then he would get it anyhow.

Therefore I gave him my Swiss wristwatch with a polite bow. He was then as though transformed, beaming with his whole visage like a child, looking at the watch, listening to it, and unable to conceal his enchantment. At once he called in the first patrol he found out on the street, lined them up before the house and gave a brief address, which we interpreted something like this: "This is the Swedish Legation's house, and this is the Attaché, an excellent man" (meaningful glance at the watch). The soldiers in the patrol nodded their assent. "Now, you are to watch the house and not let anyone in, no matter who he may be!"

So the soldiers placed themselves on watch outside the house. One month later, they were still standing there, when after many experiences we returned to Budapest for a brief visit before leaving for Sweden. By their presence they had kept the soldiers who followed them from breaking in and looting the house.

Once the fighting had stopped, I set out to look for the Russian commander of this section of the front. I eventually encountered a Major Ulas, who was sitting peacefully at breakfast with his assistant, a captain. By a stroke of luck, Ulas spoke a little German. I thought these were a couple of line officers I had chanced to meet, but actually they were officers of the NKVD, the Russian security police — something I understood only later. It turned out that they had been assigned to take charge of all foreigners, chiefly diplomats, who were encountered as the Russian troops advanced, and to move them to the rear.

I told them where the minister and the other Swedes and foreigners were staying, and I said that Consul Ekmark, Carlsson and I were living, at present, on Rose Hill. At the word "Consul," which I used more or less by chance, the major brightened, rose, and said: "*Shvedskiy Konsul*! Then we must call on him at once." I realized that a consul, in the eyes of the Russians, was an especially important person, much more important than the minister and the rest of the Swedish staff together. This should be put to use, so I vigorously encouraged the major in his desire to visit Ekmark.

We walked over to Rose Hill. Before I introduced Ekmark to both officers, I managed to let him know in a stage whisper about his high rank and station. After that, we spent an agreeable evening with our new Russian friends and emptied the last wine bottles in our pantry. Since the officers, at every toast, insisted on "bottoms up," the atmosphere eventually became very warm.

At our request, the major set up guards before several houses on Rose Hill that belonged to Swiss and Swedish citizens. The officers declared that they would come the following day and take us to the headquarters of their chief, General Pavlov, where we would remain for the time being. I tried to object that we must stay in Budapest until we could once again get in touch with the other members of our mission. Besides, I had hoped to be able to follow the advance of the troops toward the Castle Hill section and the Gellért Heights, so that I could point out to Ulas where the Swedes and the Swiss were staying. Ulas explained that civilians were not permitted to stay in or immediately behind the front lines, and so he was unable to accede to my request. But he promised to try and make sure that not a hair on the heads of the Swedish and Swiss diplomats was harmed. To help him in this, I gave him a sketch of those places where the Swedish and Swiss missions were located.

During the day, a great number of Russian units of distinctly lower quality arrived. We came through all right because of our guards and now understood how lucky we had been. As a matter of fact, we had been miraculously saved. All around us, new troops were marching in, the last pockets of resistance were cleared out, and chaos reigned. Women's screams, the death-rattles of dying men, the chattering of machine guns, the smoke of burning habitations — everything spun together into a ghastly cacophony I shall never forget.

With the Russians

The next day the Russian major, Ulas, came for Ekmark, Carlsson and me in a jeep. He took us first of all to a barber, who trimmed and shaved and otherwise smartened us up as best he could.

"When you meet the general, you have to look as neat as possible," he explained. After a long trip by jeep, we arrived in the little village of Soroksár, just south of Budapest, where we were housed in a barracks already full to bursting with Russian soldiers. We didn't consider the situation very appealing and Ekmark, in his eminence as Consul, requested that they arrange our lodgings in some other place. We would prefer to have a house to ourselves, with the possibility of a bath. The Russians were startled by our pretensions. They probably thought it strange that we were not simply grateful for having been rescued from the inferno in Budapest.

However, they set to work arranging new quarters for us. Only a single modern house existed in the village and it had been stripped by looters. So the Russians took beds, furniture, and other furnishings from the surrounding houses, pretty well emptying them, and brought it all to our house. In the end, it got to be really comfortable, and the Russians showed us their handiwork proudly. They were proudest of the bathroom. That there was no water in it, all the pipes having been bombed to bits, was a minor detail!

Thus our odyssey through the Hungarian countryside began. We followed the general's staff behind the front, and when a new lodging was scouted for the general and his officers, they always picked out a special house for us. We were treated correctly. A soldier stood day and night at his post outside our door, and when we went out for some fresh air he followed us at a suitable distance. His assignment was partly to keep his eye on us and partly to protect us from interference by other Russians. The latter part of the assignment was not least in importance, since just at this time civilians ran the continual risk of being drafted as labor by the first Russian they met.

With the Russians' permission, Carlsson and I devoted ourselves now and then to cross-country running in the vicinity. We observed with ill-concealed mirth how the Russian soldier came puffing after us in his long coat and with his rifle in hand.

None of our personal belongings had we been able to save and we had, practically speaking, only what we walked around in. But we had taken with us a vital part of the legation's equipment, the cipher machine, and we succeeded in hiding it from the Russians. In an unobserved moment, we pooled our strength to smash it to pieces with an axe in the woodshed of the farmhouse where we happened to be billeted just then. Later, during our walks, we tossed a piece here and a piece there, preferably in wells and ponds.

We received the same food as the Russians, and in time it became fairly monotonous. Tea and greasy pirozhki in the morning, cabbage soup and hash or hamburger at midday, and tea with the same kind of pirozhki in the evening. This menu never changed during the months we lived with the staff. For a little variety, we tried several times to get the Russians' permission to cook our own food in the Hungarian farmhouses where we were billeted, but they would not hear of it. The Hungarians could put poison in your food, they said. Our attempts to convince the Russians that this suspicion was exaggerated, since we had no quarrel with the Hungarian farmers, were met only with an uncomprehending shake of the head. Now we understood why the Russians never ate anything but what was prepared by their own cooks.

All this time we were worrying about the other Swedes who were still in Budapest. The Russian bomber formations passed us every day on their way to the capital, and we understood that the last bitter struggle for Buda was under way. Therefore I submitted a request to Pavlov that the Russians consider negotiations with the German commander for the safe passage of neutral missions remaining in Buda. Pavlov's reply was to the effect that they had no intention whatsoever of making any further contact with the Germans. He referred to the efforts the Russians had made earlier to get Budapest surrendered without a fight. But the Germans had treacherously shot down the Russian negotiators and so made further parley impossible.

In mid-February the staff was moved to a place called Dunavece, thirty miles south of Budapest. There we got the message that the last sections of Budapest had fallen and we waited tensely for what would happen next.

To the Russian interpreter who visited us now and then we presented our wish to be reunited quickly with the other members of the mission in Budapest.

Our intention was to return to the city so as to continue the legation's activities in some form. But General Pavlov rejected our request on the pretext that he had not yet received instructions from Moscow about what should be done with the Swedish mission.

After about a week, though, Minister Danielsson and Consular Officer von Mezey arrived from Budapest in a Russian truck. They were in a state of exhaustion. Major Ulas had kept his promise to find Danielsson and had decided to bring him and von Mezey to the place we were staying. The others remained in Budapest. Unfortunately, Ulas had come too late to the legation building on the Gellért Heights, which had already been completely looted.

Where Berg was, no one knew. The last anyone had heard of him was that he had set out to find the Russian commander to protest the attack on the legation.

Danielsson related that, after the Russians took Buda, he and the papal nuncio and the Swiss had contacted various Russian commanders, trying to work out arrangements for military guards at the different foreign legations, as well as to get identification documents for their staffs, but it had all come to nothing. The Soviets gave no consideration whatsoever to the extraterritorial rights of the diplomatic missions. Danielsson pointed out that the Swedish legation had handled the Soviet Union's interests in Hungary, and that for this reason one might expect some special consideration to be given. Yet not even this argument struck home. The Russians answered that the representative of a country which, through its iron ore deliveries to Germany, had helped prolong the war, ought to keep his mouth shut.

132

At the Swiss legation, a Cossack patrol forced its way in and demanded gold coins of the cashier. When he answered that he had none, he was beaten. He offered them a bundle of Swiss franc notes instead. These the Russians contemptuously rejected as merely paper and tore to bits. Then the legation building was looted, like all the other buildings.

Danielsson had been lucky and only lost his watch. The papal nuncio had had the gold crucifix he wore on his breast torn off. The stories about the Russians' passion for clocks were legion. There were soldiers who had wristwatches up to their elbows. One Russian was seen walking down the street with a grandfather clock he had found. Suddenly the big clock began to strike, whereupon he threw it down in a panic and with his submachine gun fired a salvo into the threatening object.

Another soldier startled people by not taking their watches, as they came to seek refuge in an air raid shelter, but instead robbing them of their eyeglasses, which he later intended to send home to his mother, who was in need of specs.

Danielsson related that the struggle for Buda had had a hideous conclusion. Late one night, the German commander had told him that the German garrison meant to fight its way out of Budapest at dawn. They believed they had found a weak spot in the Russian ring around the city and they were going to join a German relief force said to be approaching. The commander now wished to leave under the protection of the neutral embassies the 10,000 wounded German soldiers who lay in the cellars of the Castle Hill district. Is it possible that he remembered that, earlier, when we sought his protection against the arrow crossmen, he had turned us down?

The attempt to break out came the next day. Under cover of darkness and with a huge tank in the lead, the garrison marched out of the city. This was just what the Russians were hoping for. They had purposely opened a gap in the ring and now lay in ambush, waiting. The Germans were allowed to go so far that the last of their columns had left Budapest. Then the Russians opened fire with every available weapon, artillery, mortars, machine guns and rifles. The massacre was total and the Germans were annihilated to the last man.

A few days later, the German radio declared that Budapest's brave garrison had successfully fought its way out of the city and been reunited with their own!

Last Visit to Budapest

Still more time was spent in Dunavece unsuccessfully trying to get the Russians to decide what they would do with us. Time crept by, and our patience was tested. Again and again Danielsson tried to ask Pavlov what was going to happen. The answer was always the same: they were waiting for instructions from Moscow.

We passed the time playing cards. In one village we happened to find a deck of cards and Ekmark, who was an expert at bridge, taught the rest of us. It became our daily occupation for a month, making us forget for a time what we had gone through and what the future might bring. To cheer us up, every week we got the same ration of tobacco that the Russian soldiers got, with cigarette paper to roll our "papirosy." We hadn't the knack, but Danielsson knew how to roll them and taught us all.

One day the cigarette paper ran out, and we tried to roll the tobacco in newspaper, with devastating results. But the practical von Mezey found a solution. He fashioned pipes out of corn cobs and reeds in which, from then on, we smoked the good Russian tobacco with great enjoyment.

In the middle of March, we finally got a message from Pavlov that he had received instructions from Moscow. We were immediately to be sent home to Sweden by way of Rumania and Russia. There was no question of allowing the mission or, in general, any foreign representatives to remain in Hungary. After long discussions with the general, with whom we now got to speak personally for the first time, Danielsson managed to arrange for us to go into Budapest for a day to locate the other Swedes. We were given a Russian officer as our escort and were conveyed by military car to Budapest.

It was a dismal Budapest that met our eyes. During our ride through the city there was not a single whole structure to be seen. Most of the Buda side lay in ruins, and everywhere the Russians had pressed the civilian population into work clearing rubble. The Russian engineers had built a wooden bridge over the Danube where the old Margareta Bridge had stood and decorated it with huge portraits of Stalin and Molotov. Saint Joseph's Bridge, which was the least shattered of the bridges, had been repaired in a makeshift way.

The mood of the Budapest survivors was one of despair. Uncounted masses were homeless, hunger was widespread and diseases raged, especially in Buda where 50,000 bodies still lay unburied beneath the ruins. People there fled to the Pest side.

To our great joy we found the Langlets, Asta Nilsson, Margareta Bauer and Berg at the Swedish Red Cross office in Pest. Where Wallenberg was, neither Berg nor the others knew. But we hoped that after the Russians had taken Pest he had managed to get in touch with the new Hungarian government in Debrecen and might be staying there or that he might already be on the way home to Sweden.

A hasty tour of the legation building and our own quarters showed that nearly everything was bombed and looted. In particular the destruction of the main legation building was great. Here is what had happened there:

During their retreat toward the Citadel, which was located atop the Gellért Heights, the Germans entrenched themselves in the house next to the legation and from there shot the advancing Russian soldiers. The Russians then made a flanking movement and, from the back, broke into the legation building, in spite of Swedish flags, Russian-language signs, and Berg's vigorous protests. Thereafter, from the minister's apartment, they overcame the German resistance in the building next door by means of machine gun fire and hand grenades. They also went through the legation itself, checking that no Germans had hidden themselves there. No Germans did they find, but instead the minister's wine cellar. After this discovery, the Russian soldiers remained for several days in the legation, reveling their way through it all, while most of our belongings disappeared in the general turmoil. The following quotation from Berg's book may prove illuminating about the situation:

"The whole legation was like a madhouse. Singing, laughing, cursing soldiers staggered around everywhere with a bottle in one hand and a pistol in the other. The curtains were torn down, the paintings were used for targets, cabinets and closets were broken open, bottles smashed against the walls . . .

"A table in the middle of the room was filled with bottles and cans. Thirsty and hungry Russians perched all around. Each helped himself till he could hold no more, but tumbled from the chair.

"Empty bottles and cans were swept in one expansive motion to the floor. New bottles were put out, more thirsty soldiers hurried up, kicking their sleepy comrades aside . . .

"Someone found a portable phonograph in a corner, but only a single record. Over and over again the melody was played. In another corner, the field telephone rang shrilly without cease. The bottles clinked, the warmth blazed from the overheated stove, the smoke rose toward the ceiling in a fog. The Russians spewed on each other and fell down on the floor in heaps, still clinging in slumber to their submachine guns. It was nearly morning and there was simply no room for more soldiers to crowd in, before the party was over!

"Once I had assured myself that everyone in the room, including the one manning the telephone, was sleeping the deep sleep of the drunken, I took out and burned the papers the Germans and the arrow crossmen had given me for my protection. Thank God I had not been subjected to a body search at once.

"From its hiding place under the bed I took out my Russian tommygun. As great a help as it had been so many times against the arrow crossmen, it was now as great a danger to me. The Russians didn't like to find weapons on civilians. Carefully, I laid the gun on the chest of a Russian who for some reason seemed to be empty-handed. Pity I wouldn't have the chance to see his face when he later waked to find the well-polished weapon in his arms.

"Wholly exhausted by the events of the day and by the drinking I had been compelled to do that night, at last I collapsed onto my bed. With my arms around the neck of my dog like a five-year-old with his teddy bear, I was asleep already."

The legation was totally looted. The building had been ransacked from top to bottom and the safe had been blown open and emptied of its contents, among which were affidavits received from Swedish or foreign citizens under the legation's protection. The booty even included the table silver left with us earlier by the former Soviet mission.

All furnishings of any value were driven away in trucks brought there for that purpose.

One of my Hungarian friends later told us he had been ordered to stand on the shore of the Danube and destroy with an axe the antique furniture that was transported there, then throw the flinders into the river. Perhaps the legation's furniture met the same fate.

Berg and von Mezey tried to protest, but without any result. Berg then went to the Russian commander of the Buda side for help, but he explained that he could not interfere, advising Berg to talk with the Russian commander in Pest, where conditions were calmer. The latter, however, rejected Berg's plea for protection of the legation building on the pretext that the fighting in Buda was not yet over and that he could not do anything to prevent looting as long as the front-line troops remained there.

It was said that, as a reward for taking Budapest, the Russian soldiers were given free rein for three days of looting and rapine in the city. Many stories have already described the suffering that the civilian population had to undergo during these days. Much has also been written about the Russian soldiers' primitive naïveté, how they would shave themselves in toilet bowls thinking they were washbasins, and how, for lack of other strong drink, they would imbibe gasoline. Or how they could show touching feelings for small children at the same time that they could impulsively and heedlessly, especially in a state of drunkenness, shoot down innocent people.

In contrast to this stood the German killing, more cold-blooded and systematic.

We were forced to experience both kinds.

In Pest, Berg had set up a makeshift office on the premises of the Red Cross, where he had begun to shut down the legation's earlier activities. Among other things, he took the sensible step of invalidating all the protective passports and similar documents the legation had issued under the Nazi regime, since these had now served their purpose. The Russian military authorities were very irritated by continually encountering people furnished with foreign documents. The situation was not made any better by the fact that a substantial number of falsified protective passports, both Swiss and Swedish, were in circulation. Quite a few of these had ended up in the hands of arrow crossmen and others of the Nazi persuasion. They brought high prices on the black market and had contributed heavily to the inflation of foreign identification papers.

One anecdote relates that Russian Marshal Malinovski, after conquering Pest, had seen all the foreign flags waving over the buildings — including some that had no right to foreign protection — and said ironically that he had apparently come to a Swedish or Swiss city and not a Hungarian one.

Not only the protective passports but even the regular foreign passports, including diplomatic ones, were regarded with suspicion by the Russians, unless accompanied by papers issued by one of the Soviet authorities.

The Swiss diplomats, who had diplomatic passports but no Soviet documents, were jailed. A Hungarian diplomat I knew, who had defected and gone underground during the Nazi period, in spite of his diplomatic passport or perhaps just because of it, had to spend ten years in Russian prison camps. Two British secret service men who had operated in Budapest during the war identified themselves to the Russians and probably showed them rather special identification papers. They were also arrested and taken away.

Berg describes in his book the difficulties he had in establishing his identity with the Russians. They were not convinced of his identity and put lots of questions to him. How could they tell he was who he said he was? They had run into so many who declared themselves to be Swedish diplomats. How could they tell if Berg's passport was genuine? It had no Russian text. If it was true that the Swedish Legation had represented the Soviet Union in Hungary, why didn't Berg have any document from any Russian authority to support that and establish his identity?

The fact was that before our departure from Stockholm, he and I had asked the Foreign Office to get such documents for the Budapest's legation's regular personnel from the Soviet legation in Stockholm. However, those currently in charge at the Foreign Office had regarded this as completely unnecessary.

There is little profit in speculating on what could

141

have come out differently if we had received the identification we requested. We who were on the Buda side were lucky and once the fighting was over we were to a great extent treated correctly despite our lack of Russian papers. On the Pest side, on the other hand, it was considerably more difficult, and one can only guess how the Russians would have treated Wallenberg had he been equipped with an identification document issued by some Russian authority.

Since no Swedish legation official was allowed to remain in Budapest, the care of the legation's main building was entrusted to one of our local staff before we left. We further requested the Soviet authorities to arrange a separate trip home as soon as possible for those Swedish citizens who did not get permission to accompany us. A list of these citizens was given to the Russians.

The Trip Home

Our journey home started under guard on the 20th of March, 1945, first by bus to Bucharest and from there by train via Odessa, Moscow, Leningrad and Helsinki to Åbo — a trip that took almost a month. We had a Russian officer as our escort. We were treated correctly during the journey and had relatively great freedom of movement. In Bucharest we stayed a week, lodging at the Swedish legation there and at the famous hotel Athene Palace, which was then being built for the third time. Earlier, it had been a headquarters for the Germans; now, it mainly housed Hungarian Jews who had fled from Budapest.

We were especially well treated by Minister and Mrs. Reutersvärd. The minister negotiated with the Russian commander about our continued journey, and Mrs. Reutersvärd supplied us with abundant provisions for our travels through Russia.

During our stay in Bucharest, a group of Swedes from Budapest arrived. We tried to arrange for them to travel with us to Sweden, but the bureaucratic Russian commander refused. His only assignment was to see to it that our group continued the trip through the Soviet Union as planned. Other arrangements had to be made for the other Swedes. They later arrived in Sweden via Turkey.

But neither were any of us permitted to remain in Bucharest, for which I was glad. I mean that

Reuterswärd asked if I could be kept as reinforcement for his mission, something that, understandably, I was not especially longing for after the lengthy separation from my family. The Russians answered Reuterswärd's question with an absolute "nyet." There was an order to continue the transport of a certain number of persons from the Swedish Budapest legation, and that number could neither be increased nor decreased, and that was that. I dedicated a moment's gratitude to the Russian bureaucracy.

In Bucharest we had the chance, for the first time in three months, to communicate with Sweden, where they had more or less given up hope that we would come back alive. The Foreign Office had been unable to give any reassurance to our near relations, who with the greatest anxiety had followed the news of the bloody final struggle in Budapest without knowing anything of our fate. In spite of our specific request, the Russians had never informed the Swedish Foreign Office that we were in their custody. On the other hand, the Swedes had heard about Wallenberg. According to a message from Deputy Foreign Minister Dekanosov to our Moscow legation, he had been taken into protective custody by the advancing Soviet Army on the 17th of January, 1945.

The Russians had at first intended to transport us in a rail car that was like a boxcar, with hard wooden benches and no windows. After discussions here and there, however, a relatively comfortable sleeping car of the old Czarist model was placed at our disposal. It became our home for the next month. At our departure, our food supply was stolen and we had to manage for the time being with the sandwiches each of us was carrying. The tea we brewed daily had a sharp off-taste, since the water was fetched from the locomotive.

In Odessa, we had a three-day layover during which we could provision for the rest of the trip. We received permission to move freely around the city on the condition that we returned each evening to our railway car. It was exhilarating to see the American and British ships in the Odessa harbor. When, one evening, we attended a performance of "Madame Butterfly" at the opera, we were happy to see again several Dutch officers who had once asked our protection after having fled German imprisonment. We also saw Norwegian military, in uniforms very similar to the Swedish, who had been freed by the Russians from German prison camps and were staying in Odessa till their transport home could be arranged. We all breathed easier.

In Moscow, we were met by members of our Swedish mission, with Minister Söderblom in the van. He displayed evident nervousness at our arrival. Had he feared that the Russians, instead of allowing us to travel on to Sweden, would shunt our train onto the tracks to Siberia?

Söderblom took me aside, on the platform, and declared: "Remember, when you get home to Sweden — not one harsh word about the Russians!" This exhortation rang in my ears early on the morning of the 18th of April when our Finnish ship "Arcturus" headed in through the Stockholm skerries, a morning when we were all filled with a deep thankfulness at being back in freedom again.

Arriving Home

On the Stadsgård quay our families and relations met us, among them Raoul Wallenberg's mother, Maj von Dardel, who was nursing a faint hope that, in spite of everything, her son might be among us. We never suspected then that when we had passed through Moscow Wallenberg was there, confined in Lubyanka Prison.

The Foreign Office representative who was there, Gustaf Béve from Protocol, announced that the press conference would take place at the Foreign Office in an hour. The Swedish press was anxious to hear about our experiences.

We were dazed from our journey, and on the way to the Foreign Office's press bureau Söderblom's words came back: "Remember — not one harsh word about the Russians!" The mood was much the same throughout the western world, a relief that the war was ending and gratitude to the Soviets for helping to crush Nazism.

Outside the pressroom I bumped into an older colleague of mine from the political department, who gave me advice: "Tell them about your experiences — of course you're not obliged to tell everything — and answer all questions truthfully!"

We were placed on a platform before the assembled press of Stockholm and my chief, Ivan Danielsson, gave an introduction, after which he turned it over to me. I described the background of our work for the

Jews in Hungary, mentioned especially Raoul Wallenberg's great contribution, described the collapse, the German occupation, the arrow crossmen's storming of the Swedish Legation and so on, and concluded by saying: "Then the Russians came, and here we are." The reporters scribbled furiously, put no questions, and rushed away to make their press deadlines.

The next day I met Erik Wästberg on the street. "Interesting, what you had to tell us yesterday," he said. "But never have so many journalists been so tricked."

"What do you mean by that?" I asked, innocently.

"Yes, you told us so many hair-raising stories about the Nazi rampages, Raoul Wallenberg and your activities that we totally forgot to ask 'O.K., but how were the Russians?'"

At home, of course I was questioned about Raoul Wallenberg and what could have happened to him, and I never made a secret of my conviction that the Russians, after having taken him into custody, put him in a camp or prison. I was confirmed still more in my belief after Berg told me that the Russians suspected Wallenberg of being a spy, something that came out when Berg and some of Wallenberg's assistants were subjected to questioning. Further, I was told that my Swiss colleague, Secretary of Legation Feller, along with a couple of other Swiss diplomats, had been taken away and interned by the Russians. Thus it was logical to suspect that Wallenberg had suffered the same fate.

Within the Foreign Office I found little understanding for my theory and generally had the feeling that no one at home who had not been out in the war was grasping what I was talking about. Thus I accepted gratefully an offer of transfer to Cairo the following year.

Two Years Assigned to the Wallenberg Case

Two years later, in 1948, I was transferred back to the Swedish foreign office and the political section. There I was received by the section head, Sven Grafström, with the words, "Now you can take over the Raoul Wallenberg case." For a number of clues had had turned up that might indicate Wallenberg was in a Russian prison.

My conviction that Wallenberg had been taken prisoner by the Russians was to prove correct.

I myself never believed the various rumors that had been spread, just after war, concerning what had happened to Wallenberg. He was supposed to have died in an air raid, been killed by the Hungarian Nazis, escaped and been seen in disguise in Budapest, and so on. It really seemed as if certain powerful forces were trying to keep these rumors alive. It even went so far that Söderblom in Moscow, shaken by these stories, delayed the official diplomatic representations to the Russians because he was loath to exclude the possibility those rumors were true.

The foreign office had to urge Söderblom not to fall into passivity. In April he was instructed to request careful investigation, without further delay, into what had happened to Wallenberg.

When I took over the case from an older colleague, I learned that the only solid ground we had to stand on was the note from Deputy Foreign Minister Vishinsky on August 18, 1947, according to which, after careful investigation, they had established "that Wallenberg is not in the Soviet Union and that he is not known to us." The note closed with "a presumption" that during the fighting in Budapest Wallenberg had been killed or taken prisoner by Szálasi's followers.

This conclusion was no surprise, considering the rumors I have mentioned, which probably originated with the Russians or, in any case, were being spread with their approval, in an attempt to halt any further Swedish intervention.

Even if the information available to the Foreign Office during those first years could not prove that Wallenberg was still alive in Russian hands, I became more and more convinced, on taking my new assignment, that such was the case. These things supported my view:

1. On occupying Budapest, the Russians carried off and interned the Swiss chargé d'affaires as well as four other Swiss diplomatic and consular officials. After negotiations with the Soviets, the Swiss succeeded, a year later, in getting the officials released in exchange for two Soviet citizens. These were Kochetov and Novikov, who had entered Switzerland illegally and were wanted in Russia, one for theft and the other for betraying military secrets to Soviet enemies. Of special interest is the fact that, in keeping with their principle of asylum, the Swiss would probably not have handed Novikov over if getting the Swiss diplomats back had not been involved. It was a question, here, of buying "a life for a life."

Besides the two mentioned, six more Russians happened to be in prison in Switzerland, sentenced for common crimes. Even these the Swiss committed themselves to hand over at the same time, though these people did not have the same interest for the Russians.

It was natural to draw the conclusion that Wallenberg had suffered the same fate as Feller and the Swiss officials.

2. The editor, Mr. af Sandeberg, after his return in 1946 from imprisonment in the Soviet Union, had given certain information about meeting a German military man who was supposed to have been imprisoned by the Russians in the same cell as Wallenberg.

3. On arriving home, I came in contact with the Wallenberg committee that had been established by private initiative. They claimed that one of their members, the writer Rudolph Philipp, had collected clearcut evidence that Wallenberg, at least till the end of 1947 or the beginning of 1948, had been alive in a Russian prison. However, for various reasons they refused to put this material at our disposal.

4. In Lefortovskaya Prison, nine Italian diplomats had been confined. They had been exchanged for some Communists who had been imprisoned in Italy. One might suspect that some of these diplomats would be able to give information about Wallenberg. (In 1951, when I was no longer in charge of the Wallenberg case, the important testimony of the Italian diplomat Claudio de Mohr about Wallenberg's sojourn in Lefortovskaya Prison was received.)

That the Swedish government, during the first months, made no greater efforts to get Wallenberg home can be explained, to some extent, by their believing that the Russians would have a hard time locating Wallenberg because the war was still going on. They had been more worried about the other members of the mission, about whom, once Budapest had fallen, they had had no news whatever for the first three months of 1945.

In spite of everything, they had had a message from the Russians about Wallenberg, after all. When, later, we arrived home unexpectedly at the end of April, 1945, after they had almost given up hope for us, it was probably assumed that it would not be very long before Wallenberg, too, came back.

But when time passed and nothing happened, it would have been natural for the new Social Democratic government, which had come in during the summer, to take more forceful action.

It seems as though the new government soon came to feel that the Wallenberg matter was unpleasant, an especially disturbing factor in our relations with the Soviets. One almost gets the impression that Foreign Minister Undén willingly accepted Vishinsky's answer that Wallenberg was not on Russian territory.

A special committee had been set up in 1947, with Anders Örne as chairman, to examine the evidence that the writer Rudolph Philipp had in hand. They reached the conclusion that this material was trustworthy.

At a meeting in 1947 between Undén and the committee, the conflicts implicit in this matter stood out in sharp relief. The meeting is described in detail in Erik Sjöquist's clarifying book, *Affären Raoul Wallenberg* ("The Case of Raoul Wallenberg"). Therefore, I shall limit myself to reproducing one of Undén's utterances which clearly shows his attitude toward the

152

for him unpleasant question of Raoul Wallenberg's fate. In Undén's view, which was supported by Vishinsky's words, Wallenberg could have been killed in connection with the final struggle for Budapest. When Wallenberg's half-brother Guy von Dardel retorted that evidence existed that Wallenberg was alive in a Russian prison, Undén wondered what reason the Russians would have had for locking him up. Mrs. Birgitta de Wylder-Bellander, who was then the prime mover in the so-called Wallenberg Action, answered that the Russians seem to have suspected Wallenberg of being a spy. Undén then put the question that gave him away: "Mrs. Bellander, do you think Vishinsky is lying?" The answer was affirmative. "But this is terrible, this is terrible!" Undén burst out. Yet Mrs. Bellander was right. Undén's attitude is also remarkable when one remembers Vishinsky's behavior as prosecutor in Stalin's great purges of the 1930s and the preposterous accusations then directed against most of the accused.

During my continued work on the Wallenberg case, in the years 1949–1950, I noticed that Undén persisted in his negative attitude, and many times I was ready to give up. I had not gained the slightest attention at the highest level for my conviction that Wallenberg was in Russian imprisonment, or for what I thought should be done to set him free.

The then head of the political section, Sven Dahlman, was especially understanding, though, and one day he said to me: "You're going to get an opportunity to talk it over with Undén face-to-face."

The chance came when, one day at the end of 1950, I was to accompany Undén to a meeting of foreign ministers in Oslo, as his secretary. He invited me to come in and sit in his compartment during the trip.

"You have been in Budapest, Mr. Anger, and are said to have views on what has happened to Wallenberg," he began. I gave a summary of Wallenberg's and the mission's activities on behalf of the Jewish population of Budapest during the war. I spoke of why I firmly believed that Wallenberg, after having been picked up by the Russians, still remained in their custody. I concluded by saying that it was my opinion that the only language the Russians understand in a situation such as this is: meet force with force, or offer something in exchange. The Swiss and the Italians had gotten their diplomats back by exchanging them for Soviet citizens. A Dane named Hakon Dahl, who had spent six years in a Soviet prison, had been exchanged for a Russian Communist jailed in Denmark. I added that we in Sweden had given the Russians a billion crowns in credits during our 1946 trade negotiations without asking anything in return. We had had several spy cases in Sweden in which Soviet citizens were involved. Was it not conceivable that instead of expelling a spy we could hold such a person, expecting to exchange him for Wallenberg?

"The Swedish government does not do such things," Undén answered curtly and coldly, having listened to my story. The audience was at an end.

Since, after that conversation, I understood that Undén's attitude could not be changed and since I also found myself placed in an increasingly difficult position between the government and the Wallenberg committee, I went to Dahlman in January 1951 and asked to be relieved of handling the Wallenberg case.

As the reason for my request I cited the following:

As I had declared on various occasions, from the very beginning I had, like the Wallenberg committee, held the view that Wallenberg, some time after the 17th of January, 1945, had ended up in Russian imprisonment. Studies of the documents of the case had further strengthened my theory; those new clues which had recently turned up also supported the view that Wallenberg, at least immediately after the end of the war, was alive in Russian confinement.

I had continuously kept in touch with the committee. They had, in the hope that the Foreign Office would arrive at some positive result, avoided all publicity which might possibly harm this delicate matter. However, in December 1950 they had warned that their patience was at an end. The foreign minister obviously had not changed his negative attitude toward this case, and they now had no choice but to inform the press of the committee's point of view.

The reason I now wished to be relieved of the Wallenberg case was that, in many ways, I shared the committee's views on the question. It would be a conflict of interest for me to be obliged to share in composing communiques and speeches which answered articles and letters-to-the-editor from the committee that contained criticism of the Foreign Office in this matter.

Dahlman accepted my explanation for the record and told me he understood my views.

The Swedish Government's Lack of Initiative

Thus my direct involvement in Wallenberg's case came to an end. Nevertheless, like many another foreign service officer, I have, while stationed in other countries and acting on Foreign Office instructions, pursued the various leads that have turned up through the years.

When Arne Lundberg took over as Undersecretary for Foreign Affairs in 1951, the Foreign Office gained an official at the highest level who carried the question further with great energy and skill. The questioning of returning war prisoners was renewed. Lundberg's arrival in the Foreign Office coincided with the decisive testimony received from the aforementioned Italian diplomat, Claudio de Mohr. He was able to tell us that he had been confined in Lefortovskaya Prison at the same time as Wallenberg as late as 1948 and had there communicated with him by tapping on the wall. This information, as well as stories from other Italian citizens who had been imprisoned in the Soviet Union, led to our making a new Swedish representation to the Soviet government in February 1952, the first since 1947. This brought the same negative results as before.

The lack of energy and the timidity which characterized the Swedish government's behavior during the years after the war could hardly have helped but affect the Russian attitude. There is every reason to

156

believe that more forceful action from the beginning by Sweden would have led to Wallenberg's release, especially if an exchange had been proposed for some Soviet spy caught in Sweden — the scheme I referred to earlier.

One gets the feeling, reading between the lines, that even the Russians expected a proposal of this kind from Sweden. These are the lost years in the Wallenberg case. But even later there should have been and should now be possibilities, if not as great, of meeting pressure with pressure in order to get Wallenberg back or to clear up what happened to him.

The Russians' attitude toward questions such as this may be illustrated by their actions in the case of Lajmonis Niedre. He was jailed by the Russians at the end of 1978, when he was accused of espionage in his former homeland, Latvia. When he was released in March 1979, he returned to Stockholm and related the following for the press:

A top official of the Ministry of the Interior had said to Niedre that, from the Soviet standpoint, there were four alternative ways to "close the case," namely:

1. The exchange of Niedre for someone else.
2. A plea from Sweden on humanitarian grounds.
3. The Soviets to free Niedre on the grounds of his being an invalid.
4. The case to be taken up anew through a trial in Moscow.

The MVD official suggested that alternatives 1 or 2 were preferable.

Because of the state of Niedre's health, humanitarian reasons seem to have led to his release. It is easy to believe, though, that the Soviets were anxious to show accommodation because of the commotion that arose just at this time over information from the Pole, Abraham Kalinski, that Wallenberg was alive in the Soviet Union as late as 1975. Did they want to avoid creating still another irritating factor in their relations with Sweden? In that case, did this happen at Wallenberg's expense?

As is now known, the Americans showed through their embassy in Moscow great interest in the Wallenberg case as early as 1945. But the Swedes never followed up on this, and no cooperative effort on this matter was ever established between the American and Swedish missions in Moscow.

Still another example of the paralysis that characterized the Swedish behavior during the years just after the war!

Later it was established that the development of the Wallenberg matter has been very closely followed by American officials.

The Swedish journalist, Sven Strömberg, got permission in March 1979 to do research in the files of the American Department of State. He was able to find confirmation there of the American interest in Wallenberg. As late as 1974, at the request of Wallenberg's mother, Maj von Dardel, the Americans had been prepared to approach the Russians on the matter. However, these plans were cancelled by the then Secretary of State, Henry Kissinger, according to Strömberg, as a protest against Sweden's anti-American involvement in the Vietnam war.

As will be seen from the above, a tremendous responsibility weighs upon the postwar Social Democratic governments, including the coalition ministry of Erlander and Hedlund in the '50s. They have deliberately lain low and been unwilling to take any action they feared might have serious consequences for our relations with the Soviet Union. Were they, at first, so anxious to preserve our neutrality in the Cold War then starting, that Wallenberg was sacrificed on the altar of neutrality? True, the government cannot be accused of passivity during the years that followed. Countless are the clues that have been investigated and the diplomatic approaches that have been made to the Soviets, especially since 1952. But one asks oneself if a real will existed behind all the inquiries and appeals that have been made? Has it not been merely a game of make-believe in which the government, for the benefit of domestic Swedish opinion, made a show of sparing no effort in a case that they neither believed in nor wanted to believe in, because it was more comfortable that way?

"If Wallenberg is to be saved, Sweden must make a fuss all over the world," Kalinski says in an interview in the Swedish magazine *Veckojournalen* in the beginning of March 1979, and continues: "With the Russians, one must be forceful! That is the only language they understand in questions of this kind. Had the Swedish government pounded on the table earlier, you would have had Wallenberg in Stockholm long ago!"

The Erlander-Undén government should already have done that!

Why Did the Russians Arrest Wallenberg?

Naturally one wonders why Wallenberg was arrested and taken away by the Russians, while the rest of us got away. In part, it was sheer luck, at least for those of us who remained on the Buda side. It was just by chance that, just in time, I got hold of precisely that NKVD major whose assignment it was to collect the members of the Swedish diplomatic mission and convey them to safety behind the front. Neither did the Russians have any trouble establishing our identities, nor did they ever have to encounter the huge number of bearers of protective passports and other Swedish identification papers that were on the Pest side.

Further, we later learned that, at least in the first stage, there was no contact maintained between the NKVD police with Marshal Malinovsky in Pest and the corresponding organization with Marshal Tolbukhin in Buda. It was said that these two competing Russian commanders did not get along with each other especially well. The Soviet authorities in Buda were probably never briefed on what their colleagues in Pest thought of the Swedes, to our good fortune.

Thus the Russian suspicions that arose in Pest of our efforts to help the Jews were never expressed when we encountered the Russians. Therefore we were treated in a manner that was generally correct, while the Swedes on the Pest side were subjected to hard questioning about Wallenberg, whom the Russians suspected of spying. Considering the anti-Semitism in the Soviet Union, the Russians did not find it especially meritorious, either, that Wallenberg had been active in helping the Jews.

Berg, too, was somewhat under suspicion, and this is what he writes about it:

"The most deeply suspected of us seemed to be Wallenberg. For the Russians, with their understanding or, more accurately, their lack of understanding for human problems, it was completely inconceivable that Wallenberg, the Swede, had come down to Budapest to try and rescue Hungarian Jews. He must have come for some other purpose.

"In those days I was naive enough to believe that they were only accusing us of being spies for the Germans. One couldn't have known then that the Russians regarded the Americans as enemies at least as deadly as the Germans. Yet when you think about the fact that Wallenberg did come to Budapest at President Roosevelt's personal request, and that the funds at his disposal originated from the War Refugee Board in Washington, then you can understand better why the Russians regarded Raoul in particular as an American spy! And in the eyes of the Russians that was considerably worse than working for the Germans!

"One who had seen Raoul work the clock around, week after week, knew that Wallenberg had not had a moment free for any possible spying. Even though the Russians arrested increasing numbers of our assistants, no evidence was ever produced against either

161

Raoul or any of the other Swedes."

When the Russians later learned that Wallenberg had been the prime mover in the rescue of the Jews and, besides that, planned to remain in Hungary after the war to support the cause of the Jews, their mistrust of him increased. Wallenberg was already compromised, in their eyes, by having accepted American money for the aid operation. Would that financial support continue, with new, mysterious purposes? These probably were the questions the NKVD asked themselves.

In Wallenberg's plans, a new organization, the "Wallenberg Institution for Rescue and Reconstruction," would be created. Its purpose would be to take care of reuniting families, creating work opportunities for returnees, providing legal help to those injured in the war, and offering housing assistance, medical services, etc.

Of course the Russians could not imagine an independent organization of that kind in one of the territories they occupied. Add to this that the intended leader of this enterprise was a highly suspect person. The Russians themselves usually use their humanitarian organizations as a cover for espionage and probably considered it natural that other countries used similar methods.

Probably Wallenberg's reconstruction plan was, to the Russians, nothing more than an attempt at continued covert espionage. When he described his humanitarian efforts up to that time, and spoke of continuing, they probably did not believe him. Possibly the Russians have not to this day realized that they locked up an innocent person.

162

No one can say for sure what would have happened if Wallenberg had given in to our insistent pleas and, just before the fall of Budapest, joined us on the Buda side to be safer from the arrow crossmen. Perhaps he would have come home to Sweden with us. But maybe — and this is most probable — he would still have found his way back to Pest to be with his charges when the Russians came. Then the epilogue would have been no different.

It has sometimes been said that the Swedish Foreign Office expressed hesitation about his activities in Budapest and that critical voices were raised against him within the mission, too. Sjöquist writes about this in his book, where he also reports my views in the matter. I would like to repeat them here in somewhat more detail:

I think that, in the first place, we were worried that the Wallenberg operation would expand to such a scope that it would swamp us and precipitate Nazi countermoves that would have endangered the legation's continued operation. I remember returning from my visit to Sweden in August, 1944, to find that Wallenberg had set up his headquarters in the legation's main building. Thousands of Jews jammed the street outside, the courtyard, and the offices where protective passports were applied for. Understandably, the regular legation personnel were shaken by the situation. We had other assignments, too, such as Langlet's work and the protection of Swedish citizens, as well as looking after the interests in Hungary of a number of countries. Wallenberg realized this. When he had completed his organization, he located the greater part of his operations on the Pest side, where his various offices were set up and where, later, the Swedish houses offered refuge to bearers of the protective passport. Wallenberg chose to establish himself in Pest because the greater part of the Jewish population lived there. It was in Pest, too, that the Nazis had set up the general ghetto. Besides that, there was information circulating that the Russians intended to take that section of the city first, whereby Wallenberg and his charges would more quickly have reached safety.

The question continually came up of how many protective passports we dared to issue. We had an agreement with the Szálasi government for the approval of 5,000 such passports and the right to house the bearers of such passports under our protection in the Swedish houses.

Obviously, the number did not stay at that level. Many times that number of passports were secretly being issued, all the while, but these were limited to those persons who could show some kind of tie to Sweden. Had we given in to the temptation to issue protective passports to just anybody among the Jewish population, the papers definitely would have lost their value. Besides, the Nazis would then have realized that we were sabotaging the agreement for a limited number, and they would have taken such measures that we would no longer have been able to help.

These and other difficult questions of judgment were discussed continually with Wallenberg and he was as conscious as we that the legation's continued operation must not be hazarded. When we had come to general agreement on the guidelines, our collab-

164

oration in the work went painlessly and Danielsson never had any objections to signing the thousands of protective passports. None of us hesitated about the effort to aid the Jews in itself. This can be seen from the fact that we, as related earlier, freely chose to stay to the end, so that the arrow crossmen would not celebrate our departure by blowing the Swedish houses and their occupants to bits.

We understood clearly that we were staying on at our own risk and that the Foreign Office, should anything happen to us, would be able to wash its hands of us. We had been perfectly free to travel home. At the same time, we were conscious of humanitarian interest back in Sweden and knew that the operation must not end in a catastrophe.

Seen from a political standpoint, the Wallenberg operation fitted into the picture, too, since in the last stages of the war the Swedish government was anxious to show as many examples as possible of neutral Sweden's help in rescuing victims of Nazism.

So the question came down to how far Wallenberg and we dared to bend the bow when we had no support from home. True, it was bent to the breaking point, and probably all of us were aware that, in the worst event, it could end up costing all of us our lives. Good triumphed, however, and the work was enabled to continue right up to the end with utterly heroic contributions, especially by Wallenberg.

The arrow crossmen came too late to liquidate us. The work was already accomplished and the Russians took over.

Continuing Actions

Wallenberg's unknown fate has preoccupied Swedish public opinion from the end of the war to this very day. It has come to be a question of decency to find out what happened to a man who, on official Swedish assignment, rendered such unique service to mankind.

Under the skillful leadership of Undersecretary Leif Leifland, the Foreign Office continues to pursue the new leads that turn up. With great seriousness, Leifland set to work on the aforementioned testimony of Abraham Kalinski at the end of 1978, according to which Wallenberg was seen in various Soviet prisons during the '50s, '60s and 70s, that is, after the year 1947 when, according to the Soviet authorities, he is supposed to have died. This information led to a new representation to the Soviet government in January, 1979.

The Soviets, in their reply, maintained that the new information did not alter their earlier answer that Wallenberg died in 1947. In a press bulletin from the Foreign Office after that reply, it was said that the Swedish government does not regard Raoul Wallenberg's case as closed by this Soviet answer but plans to continue its effort to clear up what his fate has been. In contrast to the earlier situation, especially in the years right after the war, a trusting cooperation now takes place between the government and the Wallenberg committee, which consists of Wallenberg's closest relatives and a number of others who, wherever they may be, have worked through the years for Wallenberg's cause. Nina Lagergren and Guy von Dardel have been tireless in this work and deserve all possible support.

Committees have also been established in foreign countries by persons who were rescued by Wallenberg or for some other reason have become interested. In Jewish circles in the United States, powerful forces are in motion, attempting to gain certainty about Wallenberg. The circumstance that the United States at one time financed the Swedish aid effort through its War Refugee Board is the mainspring in the effort to engage the American government in action for Wallenberg. Four American senators have become leaders of an action group and have declared that if Wallenberg still lives, everything possible must be done to assure his freedom. At this writing, word has been received that the Americans have made a representation to the Soviet Embassy in Washington. In Great Britain, a group in Parliament is working for Wallenberg and in Israel, the prosecutor of the Eichmann trial, Gideon Hausner, is a driving force. Besides this, the "Nazi hunter" Simon Wiesenthal is at work on the case in Vienna, in Israel and elsewhere.

During my various tours abroad after the war, in both Europe and the United States and even as far away as Australia, I have met Hungarian Jews who were rescued by Wallenberg. I have often been asked to lecture on the Swedish efforts in Hungary, most recently in Sydney a few years ago before the Jewish association, B'nai B'rith. The chairman said that I had been invited to tell about a terrible epoch in the history of the Jews. It was vital that the world be re-minded of these events and that every effort be made to prevent any possible recurrence.

After my talk came an opportunity for questions, but only deep silence ensued. After a moment, a man rose and said: "I have no questions to ask. I can only testify that we have now heard the truth about what happened. I was there. I have been waiting twenty-five years for the chance to thank Wallenberg, to thank the Swedes for my life. Here is my protective passport." And he held up a passport signed by Danielsson.

In this connection, I have also encountered Jews who endured suffering that one cannot understand a human being surviving. I know a woman who first had to witness the brutal murder of her husband and child and then was shot down and buried alive. She was miraculously rescued and today lives a normal life, has remarried and has children again.

There are men who, in their teens, were forced by the Nazis to break the gold teeth out of the mouths of their dead relatives — men who subsequently found a way to work, make a family, and adjust to a normal life.

One can only be amazed at man's boundless will to live, his spiritual and physical endurance.

I am often asked whether I believe that Wallenberg is still alive. And I answer: "Of course I do, at least until it can be proved otherwise." "We must not give up," said Foreign Minister Blix in an interview in May, 1979, in connection with Kalinski's revelations, and he continued: "In cases such as this, a principle of Swedish negotiation is that we assume they are alive until we see that convincing evidence exists that they have died."

I have met German diplomats who sat in Russian prisons for about ten years and came through it. True, that is not so long a period as in Wallenberg's case. However, he had an unusually strong physique and an impressive strength of spirit. I am angered by those writers who, on undefined grounds, try to prove that Wallenberg was killed by the Nazis at the end of the war or died in Lubyanka Prison in 1947, in accordance with the Russian version of the story. One wonders what purpose such assertions have served?

In his excellent book, *Raoul Wallenberg – Fakta kring ett öde* ("Raoul Wallenberg — The Facts About His Fate"), Fredrik von Dardel, Wallenberg's stepfather, tells of those accounts given by returning prisoners of the Soviets in which Wallenberg is said to have died at various places and times. Every one of these tales has proven to be untrustworthy, von Dardel says, and can be suspected of originating with the Soviet authorities. Considerably greater trust can be placed in the testimony that has been given by impartial, reliable persons that Wallenberg was in Butyrki Prison in January, 1951, in Vladimir Prison during the '50s, and in a mental hospital in the Soviet Union during January, 1961 — this according to von Dardel.

Fredrik von Dardel and his wife Maj passed away in February, 1979, not long after yet another negative answer from the Soviets concerning their son. For over thirty years they had fought for him. His parents are no more, but the struggle must not be abandoned. It shall continue until Raoul Wallenberg is released or certainty has been achieved about his fate.

Hungary Once More

On October 23, 1956, the Hungarian Revolution broke out. I was then serving at the Swedish Embassy in Vienna and once again had to experience at close range a shattering phase of Hungarian history.

Life in Vienna in those days was greatly affected by the events taking place in that neighboring country. The Viennese followed the events with anxiety. Despite Austria's neutral policy, neither on the official nor on the individual level was there any attempt to conceal where their sympathies lay. The shipment of food, clothing, bandages and medicines through the border stations that now lay open was arranged. Vienna came to be a marshaling point for the humanitarian aid efforts of other countries.

One of the first to arrive was a Swedish Red Cross convoy, some ten vehicles under the direction of Major Jan Tillander. At the news of the Hungarian Revolution, the convoy had been organized overnight, and they had driven straight through to Vienna without stopping. On one of the last days of October it arrived outside the embassy and Tillander asked to be briefed on the situation.

I explained that, to the best of our knowledge, there was no fighting going on in the area between Vienna and Budapest, and the road lay open for traffic. The Red Cross vehicles continued and reached Budapest with their valuable cargo of medicines, bandages and blood plasma, of which the freedom

170

fighters were especially in need. But their return trip was delayed, since the women and children of the Swedish mission were to come back with them. Five miles from the Austrian border the convoy was stopped by a Russian troop unit which had now taken back the control of the highway connections between Vienna and Budapest.

For several days we remained in the dark about what had happened to the Red Cross convoy. It was rumored, among other things, that they had been fired on by the Russians. I reproached myself severely for not dissuading Tillander from continuing to Budapest. However, through an official representation via our embassy in Moscow we succeeded in getting the Russians to release the convoy, and everyone was able to continue to Vienna unharmed.

Here it should be mentioned that Swedish Radio's Kurt Andersson went along with the convoy into Budapest. As the first foreign radio correspondent on the scene, he was able to give Sweden as well as the rest of the world a direct report from the Budapest radio station about the situation there. He later became a legend by continuing to speak from the city's radio studio through the final struggle for Budapest to the very end.

My then chief in Vienna, Ambassador Sven Allard, was widely known for his deep knowledge of conditions in the eastern countries, and the Austrian foreign ministry was now eager to seek his advice and learn his views about the situation in Hungary.

One day in the beginning of November, he returned from a meeting with the Austrians and told me that they looked upon the situation as very grave.

The Austrian officer who had spoken said that an enormous concentration of Russian troops had taken place along the Hungarian-Austrian border. In his military judgment this could mean only one thing: that the Russians were preparing to invade Austria during the next two days.

"What do you think?" Allard asked me. I realized that he had already made up his mind but that he wanted to hear the views of a younger colleague. "I don't think it's so," I answered. "There must be some other reason for the Russians' troop concentration. The Russians can't reasonably risk a third world war. The Americans are not going to stand idly by while the Russians occupy Austria. We know that from the American ambassador."

"I share your opinion," said Allard. "But, just for safety's sake, check that the shelter in the garden is in working order and arrange to spend the next couple of nights here in the embassy just in case anything should happen."

Would I once again, after eleven years, have to experience the horrors of war? I could not really believe it, but on the way home that day I bought some canned food, which I handed to my startled wife.

The Soviets never attacked Austria. Several days later we learned the explanation for the major build-up on the border. The Russians had decided to crush the Hungarian freedom fighters by force of arms. To cover their rear and prevent any possible intervention by the western powers, something the Russians with their usual mistrustfulness could not exclude, they concentrated their forces on the threshold of Hungary.

Ever since the beginning of the fighting, we had had no direct contact with the mission in Budapest. True, Tillander's Red Cross convoy had returned from there with the women and children, but they had left before the Russians attacked the city.

Therefore, with Allard's permission, we notified the Foreign Office that I was willing to travel to Budapest to investigate the situation and, if necessary, assist the mission there for a time. Thinking of my experiences in the last war, though, I put as a condition that the Foreign Office was to arrange for permission from the Russians, a safe-conduct for me. The Foreign Office's response was rather startling. They accepted my offer but regarded it as most sensible under the circumstances to transfer me to Budapest.

I considered that I had already done my share in Budapest and that there ought to be others in the Foreign Office who were in line for such a post. Yet when I told my wife about it, she answered spontaneously: "Naturally you'll do your duty, and this time the baby and I will go along. I don't want us to be separated again like during the war, when we were apart for nine months and for a long time I didn't know whether you were alive or dead."

I conveyed her wishes to the Foreign Office, which got cold feet at the thought of sending a family with a child to Budapest under the conditions prevailing and so refrained from transferring me there. On the other hand, they were willing for me to travel by myself and help the mission out for a few weeks.

Just when my Russian safe-conduct had arrived and I was ready to leave, Barbro Alving of the Stockholm daily *Dagens Nyheter* called me up.

"I hear that you've received the Russians' permission to travel to Budapest," she said. "In that case, I and Lars Orup are coming along." Barbro and Orup belonged to a group of journalists who had collected in Vienna from different countries and were now trying to get into Hungary to do reportage. A few reporters had managed to get themselves in while the freedom fighters were holding the borders open but, now that the Russians had taken over again, entry was considerably more difficult. So my counterquestion to Barbro Alving was: "Have you got the Russians' permission?"

"No, but we have the Hungarians'."

When I objected that it was altogether too risky for them to come along, and that I probably would not be able to help them in case they were arrested by the Russians, she paid no mind. "We'll travel at our own risk," she said very firmly. And that was that.

On the morning of November 26, we met at the Austrian border station Nickelsdorf. We formed a little convoy of three cars. I took the lead, followed by Sigvard Kruuse from the Budapest mission, who had come to Vienna with the Red Cross convoy, and Alving and Orup came last.

I had equipped all the vehicles with Swedish flags on the windshields, and my Russian safe-conduct was in readiness.

At the Hungarian border station Hegyeshalom we were stopped by Russian military. On opposite sides of the road, two Russian tanks were entrenched, with their cannon aimed at Austria.

I showed my passport and my Russian safe-conduct and, with a gesture back toward the two other cars, I spoke those Russian words I had not uttered since my first meeting with the Russians on Rose Hill in Budapest, in February 1945: "Shvédskoye Posólstvo," that is, Swedish Legation. The Russian commander saluted and let the cars go by. No inquiry was made regarding the baggage or the purpose of the trip. The maneuver was repeated, with the same happy outcome, at the six more Russian barriers we had to pass through to get to Budapest!

At the first of these Russian checkpoints, an episode occurred that engraved itself in my memory. While the Russian commander was occupied with my papers, we saw a Hungarian refugee family, a man and wife with two children, who, a hundred yards from us, ran across a field in the direction of the Austrian border. Two Russian soldiers set out after them. When the Russian officer became aware of the situation, however, he called them back with his whistle, and the Hungarian family could continue toward freedom. Probably it was our presence that saved them because the Russian thought it embarrassing to intervene while we were watching.

We found Budapest battered and ravaged after the fighting. The ruins were being cleared away, and overturned streetcars and buses were still blocking traffic. Famine threatened, and outside the grocery shops long queues snaked down the streets. During the war, Buda had been hardest hit; now it was Pest's turn. The worst destruction occurred on Sunday morning, November 4, when the Russians, after having held out the prospect of negotiations with the freedom fighters, treacherously broke the cease-fire and began the artillery bombardment of Pest from the heights of Buda. Building after building was blown to bits. The Russians were no longer taking any chances when it came to crushing "the rebellion."

Kruuse and I separated from Alving and Orup. Their Budapest reporting resulted in many widely noticed articles and radio programs in Sweden. At the legation, I found our chargé d'affaires, Stig Rynell, and his aides in good shape. I heard first-hand descriptions of the fighting and of the heroic Hungarian people's struggle against the superior Russian forces.

Once more the unbelievable strength of the Hungarian will to freedom had been demonstrated. Desperate after years of terror and oppression from not only the Hungarian Communist Party and the secret police but also the occupying forces, the Hungarians took up arms. It was an uprising and a national rallying without equal in the history of the nation, comparable with the rebellion against the Austrians in 1848 under the folk hero, Lajos Kossuth. Students and laborers, old and young fought side by side at the barricades while the farmers took care of supplying them with food. The Russians were taken by surprise and at first abandoned the field. For eleven days, Hungary was free again and the people were masters in their own house. But no one knew how long it would last.

At the legation, they were almost the most impressed by the fighting of the younger schoolboys. They operated in teams. One team threw paving stones into the tracks of the Russian tanks. As soon as a tank was halted, a team came running from another direction and threw bottles of gasoline, the so-called Molotov cocktails, at the tank, with terrible effect. Often the old grandparents were sitting in a doorway filling the bottles. These boys had been fostered in the Communist doctrine ever since they had begun school. Now they turned these weapons against their Russian teachers.

I met my friends from the 1944 resistance against the Nazis. Now they were fighting the Russians, and they allowed themselves no illusions about the future. But they just could not stand oppression any longer. "That's why we rebelled, and during those eleven days the Hungarian people got back their soul," they said.

The legation's housekeeper, Annus, told us of her happiest moment — when she together with other citizens of Budapest pulled down Stalin's statue with a long rope. I saw my old friend, Ferenc Pirkner, the head of the Hungarian branch of the Swedish SKF, the well-known Swedish ball-bearing company, which continued to operate in Hungary for some years after the war. He was now planning a second rebuilding of his bombed-out factory. The motto everywhere was: "We shall never surrender." This attitude, stamped with an indomitable longing for freedom, was typical of everyone. The memory of the Hungarian people's folk heroes, Ferenc Rákoczy, Lajos Kossuth and the poet Sándor Petöfi, was invested with new life. Wallenberg's name still lived among many of the people of Budapest. Countless were the expressions of gratitude I now received from those he had rescued. Yet no one could explain what had become of him.

I saw the street in Pest that had been named after him. It was the street where the Swedish houses were located and had formerly been called Phoenix Street.

After my return to Austria in December, a new

phase of the Hungarian tragedy began: the great refugee exodus to Austria. In the space of one month, 175,000 Hungarians managed to leave their country before the iron curtain was slammed shut again. Austria mobilized all imaginable resources to receive them.

The greater part of the refugees were subsequently admitted to other countries of western Europe, the United States, Canada, and Australia. Sweden accepted 5,000.

In Vienna, various UN agencies, volunteer organizations and the International Red Cross supported the Austrians by transporting the refugees and by sending aid shipments to Hungary. As the leader of the Red Cross effort, the Swede Henrik Beer served with his well-known skill and efficiency.

One day, Anna Hägglöf, the wife of our Swedish ambassador in London, arrived to offer her services. When the Red Cross could not find a way to employ her, she came up to the embassy and asked me to arrange for a job. My colleague, Erik Braunerhielm, who was involved in the transportation of the 5,000 refugees to Sweden, proposed that Anna Hägglöf go along with them as "bus hostess" between Vienna and Sassnitz. She accepted the assignment gladly and carried it out with great skill and sensitivity. Within a short time, Anna Hägglöf had become extraordinarily popular with the refugees. High officials suddenly discovered her talents and offered her the post of head of the kitchen in the largest refugee camp, Traiskirchen, south of Vienna. To this camp came Gunnar Hägglöf, too, in December, 1956, to spend Christmas with her and the refugees.

Well-known is the rather comic episode that Hägglöf relates in his book, *Minnen inför framtiden* ("Memories Before the Future"), when the then vice-president of the United States, Nixon, came to visit the camp.

Hägglöf writes: "Right in the middle of preparations for the evening meal, Nixon arrived, surrounded by a swarm of photographers and reporters. Hungarian refugee children had to be trotted out to be embraced by Nixon. Ragged refugees had to relate their sufferings while the vice-president patted them on the shoulder consolingly. The whole thing was a huge charade, calculated to be spread across page one of the American newspapers. All this time, the Red Cross' staff worked patiently to be able to serve the food at the appointed time to the thousands of refugees who were already lining up impatiently in the slush of the camp yard. But Nixon and his crowd of photographers only went on and on in the glare of the limelight. At last, Anna went up to them to tell them it was high time they got out of the kitchen. But when the vice-president and the others made not the slightest move to withdraw, Anna got mad and advanced, brandishing her ladle. 'Out,' she cried, 'out! this very minute!' Then Nixon finally slunk away."

Anna Hägglöf was as though created for the job of helping people in distress. No one has better described this side of her nature than Barbro Alving, whom Hägglöf quotes in his book, *Engelska år* ("English Years"). I reproduce the following passage: "She raced to Vienna. Oh yes, one may say. Wives of high-ranking diplomats who rush around on such occa-

sions and for a few days dabble in aid to refugees —
we've seen all that before.

"Anna Hägglöf (with lungs scarred by tuberculosis,
which she never utters a word about) stood through
many nights by that dark, legendary border canal
where the stream of refugees crossed. I know how it
was there, at Andau, and elsewhere: frosty vapors
rising out of the dark swamp, glimmering flashlights,
bitter cold. Anna Hägglöf's job, like that of others: to
pull people up out of the water, to carry the injured
and fainting ones, to get some food into them and
calm their hysteria. For three weeks she labored
there. Then for three months at the largest receiving
camp, Traiskirchen. I'm not going to replay here the
gray and tense scenes of camp life then, with tens of
thousands homeless and hopeless. There's no need
to. But three months show that a person is serving in
earnest."

Andau, which Barbro Alving mentions, is the place
on the border east of Vienna where three-fourths of
the Hungarian refugees found their way to freedom.
To get a picture of the situation, Allard and his wife
Maggie and I drove there one evening in the middle
of December, 1956. We came up to the four-yard-
wide Eisner Canal at Andau, where we knew many of
the refugees arrived. By the canal stood two young
men, turning blue with cold, an American and an
English student.

"What are you doing here?" I asked.

"Well, we were studying at the Sorbonne and we
heard about the Hungarian Revolution and figured
we ought to make a contribution," was the answer.
"We got us a rubber boat in Vienna and when the

refugees come, we help them across in the boat, so they don't have to wade in the ice-cold water. They generally get here around three in the morning. We've been here every night for the past week. Just wait and you'll see."

He was quite right. Around three, the refugees appeared as dark shadows on the opposite side of the canal, and the two students set to work. Crying infants got candy from the Englishman, and their elders, a swig of Hungarian apricot brandy from the American, along with a handshake and an emphatically welcoming "*servus*."

Touching scenes took place when these refugees reached Austrian soil. Many fell to their knees and thanked God for having been saved, and most of them wept for joy. We were deeply moved at meeting these people who had been forced to leave their homes, their country and everything behind them, to face an uncertain future.

On the way home, I proposed to Allard that we try to arrange to handle transporting the refugees to the first of the Austrian receiving camps, which lay six miles from Andau, a substantial distance to go on foot in an exhausted condition. Maggie Allard, who had for many years taken an active role in helping needy Hungarians, supported my proposal. So that the embassy would not be advertised as the origin of the planned transportation, we turned to the Swedish organization Save the Children and proposed that they put a Volkswagen bus and some personnel at our disposal. That is what happened, and at the embassy we worked in shifts to help collect the refugees.

I came along to Andau on the first sally to collect

refugees, accompanying Col. Lemmel's wife, Margit, who was one of the leaders of Save the Children in Sweden. She had come to Vienna to take over the transport.

In Andau, the bus was parked on a little hill near the border and I headed for the canal, where I found the two students again. The refugees arrived at the same time of night as before, and the same scenes took place. I led the group of refugees to the bus and the waiting Margit Lemmel, who efficiently carried out shuttle service between Andau and the receiving camp.

Among the refugees were several Jews whom Wallenberg and we had once rescued with Swedish protective passports.

An elderly Hungarian woman fell, weeping, into my arms. She had recognized me from that day at the end of 1944 when, at the railway station in Budapest, I succeeded in rescuing a number of Jews from deportation. She was one of them!

It was a strange and touching reminder of the days in Hungary with Raoul Wallenberg.

Bibliography

Berg, Lars G. Vad hände i Budapest. Stockholm 1949.

Biss, Andreas. A Million Jews to Save. South Brunswick 1975.

Braham, R. L. The Hungarian Jewish Catastrophe. New York 1962.

von Dardel, Fredrik, Raoul Wallenberg — fakta kring ett öde. Stockholm 1970.

Encyclopedia Judaica, Volumes 4 and 18.

Isakson, Börje. Omöjligt uppdrag: Raoul Wallenbergs kamp i Budapest 1944–1945. Falun 1975.

Langlet, Valdemar. Verk och dagar i Budapest. Stockholm 1946.

Lévai, Eugene. Black Book on the Martyrdom of Hungarian Jewry. Zurich 1948.

Lévai, Eugene. Raoul Wallenberg — hjälten i Budapest. Stockholm 1948.

Lukacs, John. 1945 Year Zero. New York 1978.

Macartney, C. A. October Fifteenth. Edinburgh 1961.

Morse, Arthur D. While Six Million Died. New York 1967.

Philipp, Rudolph. Raoul Wallenberg, Diplomat, Kämpe, Samarit. Stockholm 1946.

Reitlinger, Gerald. The Final Solution. London 1953.

Sabille, Jacques. Lueurs Dans La Tourmente. Paris 1956.

Sjöquist, Eric. Affären Raoul Wallenberg. Stockholm 1974.

Syrkin, Marie. Blessed is the Match. New York 1947.

Ullein-Reviczky, Antal. Guerre Allemande, Paix Russe. Neuchâtel 1947.

Utrikesdepartementet (Swedish Foreign Office): Raoul Wallenberg. Dokumentsamling jämte kommentar rörande hans fångenskap i Sovjetunionen. Stockholm 1957.

Utrikesdepartementet (Swedish Foreign Office): Raoul Wallenberg. Dokumentsamling rörande efterforskningarna efter år 1957. Stockholm 1965.

Villius, Elsa & Hans. Fallet Raoul Wallenberg. Stockholm 1966.

Vörös, Marton. Även för din skull. . . Stockholm 1978.

Weissberg, Alex. Desperate Mission: Joel Brand's Story as told by Alex Weissberg. New York 1958.

Wulf, Joseph. Raoul Wallenberg. Berlin 1958.

Index

186

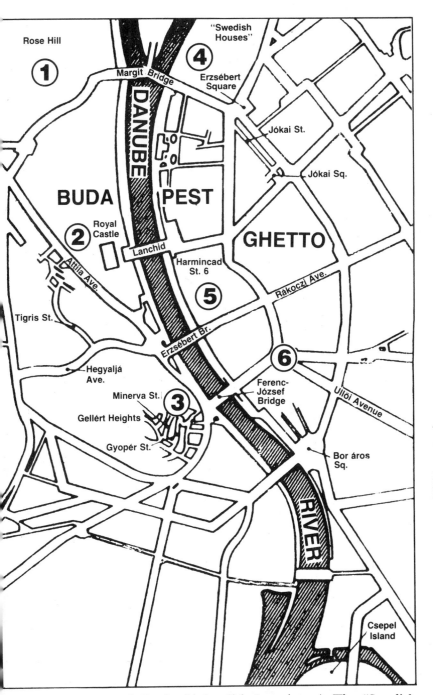

1. Rose Hill. 2. Royal Castle. 3. Swedish Legation. 4. The "Swedish Houses." One of the streets in the vicinity now bears Raoul Wallenberg's name. 5. Harmincad Street No. 6, Wallenberg's last known residence in Budapest. 6. Üllöi Avenue No. 2, Wallenberg's "headquarters".

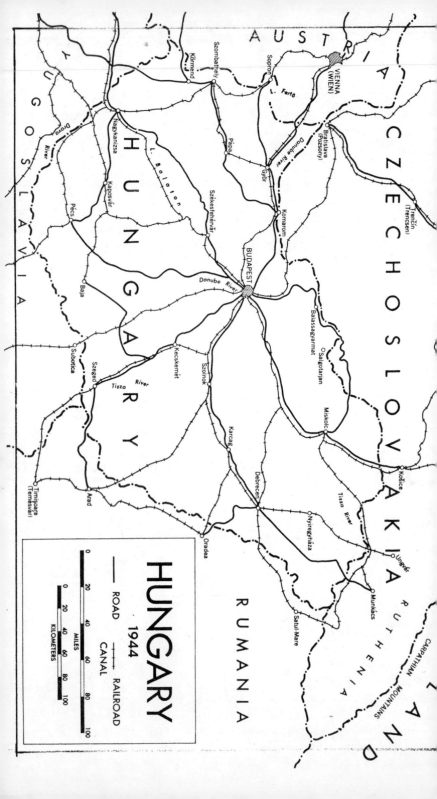

...Ő KIRÁLYI KÖVETSÉG.

Ezen oltalomlevéllel ellátott helyiség a budapesti

SVÉD KIRÁLYI KÖVETSÉG

védelme alatt áll.

Budapest, 1944. augusztus 1.

KÖNIGLICH SCHWEDISCHE GESANDTSCHAFT.

Die mit diesem Schutzbriefe versehenen Räumlichkeiten stehen unter Obhut der

KÖNIGLICH SCHWEDISCHEN GESANDTSCHAFT IN BUDAPEST

Budapest, 1. August 1944.

Original document issued by the Royal Swedish Legation for the purpose of claiming exterritoriality for the apartments and shops of Swedish-protected persons

About the Author

Per Anger was born in Göteborg, Sweden, in 1913. Upon graduating from Uppsala University in 1939 he entered the diplomatic service and was assigned to the Swedish Foreign Office in Stockholm. His first foreign assignment was in 1940 when he joined the staff of the Swedish Embassy in Berlin. He was transferred to Budapest in 1942. There as an attaché in the Embassy he became involved in the rescue of the persecuted Hungarian Jews then being carried on by several neutral governments and by the International Red Cross.

In July 1944, Raoul Wallenberg arrived in Budapest and Per Anger became his close and devoted collaborator in the noble humanitarian mission of saving Hungarian Jews from deportation to the gas chambers of Auschwitz.

Raoul Wallenberg saved about 25 thousand Jews directly and another 70 thousand indirectly. In a tense dramatic account Per Anger relates their experiences in Budapest during those fateful years 1944–45. He recounts his association with Raoul Wallenberg in his rescue work and tells of Wallenberg's tragic fate after his arrest by the Russians.

After the war Per Anger was assigned to the Swedish Embassies in Cairo, Addis Ababa, Paris, and the Consulate General in San Francisco. His most recent assignment was as Sweden's Ambassador to Ottawa. He retired in December 1979 after forty years of distinguished diplomatic service to his country.

Ambassador Per Anger has been married to Elen Wikstrem Anger for 37 years. They have a married daughter and two sons.